Hannah's Journey
To Purpose

Hannah's Journey To Purpose

Sandra (Lott) Smith

Your New Life Ministries LLC

"And whenever the time came for Elkanah to make an offering, he would give portions to Peninnah his wife, and to all her sons and daughters. But to Hannah, he would give a double portion, for he loved Hannah, although the Lord had closed her womb."
(I Samuel 1:4-5)

This book is dedicated to my Heavenly Father, who has been so very faithful to me. He has been faithful through all of my bad choices, slow learning, not seeing or understanding, and a lot of unnecessary worry and complaining. He has been faithful through my impatience when I did not understand what He was doing in my life and in me. He never gave up on me and saw in me a servant of God whom He could use for His purpose and glory. I thank Him and praise Him for His unconditional love!

This book is also dedicated to Patricia Williams who was a very good friend. She has gone home to be with the Lord and still makes a difference. She had cancer and she did not allow that to define her and stop her devotion to God which clearly showed. She persevered just like Hannah. The light of Jesus shone through her in her daily life. She was full of love and compassion and had a spirit of grace that drew people to her. Her life was a witness, which always provided her the opportunity to witness Christ. May I live by her example.

Contents

Introduction

Everyone loves a good love story, and I don't think many people would see one in "The Lord closed her womb." Reading those words, I wondered why. Why did the Lord close her womb? Maybe Hannah had sinned in some way which resulted in the Lord closing her womb. As I read how much Elkanah loved Hannah, believing that she sinned in some way did not seem to be a possibility. In finding an answer to my question all I could hear in my spirit was, "Dig deeper."

This book is about the love of Elkanah for his wife, Hannah. As he saw Hannah weep for children, his love was so great that to him, her happiness was more important than having children. This book is also about God's love for Hannah in that He chose to use her to give birth to Samuel for His purpose. The whole Bible is God's love story for mankind, and as I began to dig deeper, I saw another part of God's love story for us unfold. God Almighty is the Ancient of Days, who always was, is, and will be eternally. He is all-knowing, ever-present, the Alpha and the Omega, beginning and end. He is all-powerful, a Mighty God, and it is very humbling when He chooses to use any of us for anything for His love to shine through us to others. Wow! Every time He uses me, the same question arises within my heart: "Why me, Lord? Who am I that you should want to use me?" That is just one part of His love story for all of us. Even in the middle of our situation when we cannot imagine how any good can come of it or if we will make it through, God already knows and has faith in us to persevere.

"O Lord, You have searched me and known me. You know my sitting down and my rising up; You are acquainted with all my ways. For there is not a word on my tongue, but behold, O Lord, You know it altogether. You have hedged me behind and before and laid Your hand upon me. Such knowledge is too wonderful for me; It is high, I cannot attain it. Where can I go from Your Spirit? Or where can I flee from Your presence? If I ascend into heaven, You are there; If I make my bed hell, behold, You are there. If I take the wings of the morning, and dwell in the uttermost parts of the sea, even there Your hand shall lead me, and Your right hand shall hold me. If I say, 'Surely the darkness shall fall on me,' even the night shall be light about me; indeed, the darkness shall not hide from You, but the night shines as the day; The darkness and the light are both alike

to You. For You formed my inward parts; You covered me in my mother's womb. I will praise You, for I am fearfully and wonderfully made; marvelous are Your works, and that my soul knows very well. My frame was not hidden from You, when I was made in secret, and skillfully wrought in the lowest parts of the earth. Your eyes saw my substance, being yet unformed. And in Your book, they all were written, the days fashioned for me, when as yet there were none of them. How precious also are Your thoughts to me, O God! How great is the sum of them! If I should count them, they would be more in number than the sand; When I awake, I am still with You." (Psalm 139:1-18)

The trials you go through are what He uses to give you experience, to draw out of you the passions and purpose He has for you–ones that you might not otherwise have ever thought of or ever desired, just like Hannah.

When Jesus was called to the aid of Lazarus, Mary, and Martha's brother, He waited two more days before He went to them. Why was that? We ask the same thing when we are going through a tough trial and the pain is almost beyond bearable. We want "microwave" answered prayers, and do not want to wait, and when the trials take longer than we like, we throw temper tantrums. One reason the Lord might have stayed longer is that He would have been glorified in healing Lazarus but was even more glorified in raising him from the dead! "For I know their works and their thoughts. It shall be that I will gather all nations and tongues, and they shall come and see My glory." (Isaiah 66:18) Another reason might be that the miracles He was performing were indeed overwhelming, and the Israelites who were used to following the letter of the Law, or at least attempting to, needed the visible miracles as eye openers so to speak.

"When Jesus heard that, He said, 'This sickness is not unto death, but for the glory of God, that the Son of God may be glorified through it.'" (John 11:4)

When Jesus called Lazarus to "come forth," He called others to remove the grave clothes. He could have done it, but He used others, so they could be a part of the miracle. He did this, so they could experience the love and power of God in raising Lazarus from the dead and know that He is the Son of God.

When the journey gets rough, remember Hannah and what the Lord brought about for her, and do not give up!

"LAZARUS COME FORTH"

As you called out to Lazarus, "Come forth," you call out to us.

You speak to the inner sanctuary of our heart and soul, the veil is removed our spiritual eyesight is restored.

Your truth is made known and blindness is no more.

The grave clothes fall away, and our hearts are born again.
We are made new in the likeness of Christ.
Our sins are forgiven; our soul is redeemed.
The chains of bondage are gone, and we are forever freed.
Our grave clothes are gone; we are no longer dead but born again!
In your hands, our hearts and souls are forever there to stay.

Our Spirit is renewed and shines like the Son.
Our hearts are bound no more but feel light and free!
Our God is glorified for all the world to see!
You call out to us, "Come forth! Be born again and be set free!"

Jesus becomes alive in us when we are being used in our calling in the purpose He has for us. He is life, and when we are using His life, His love, and His power within us for others, we feel it grow within us. When I worship and praise Him, and allow the Holy Spirit to speak through me, to witness, to serve, to be His vessel to encourage and to heal others, I feel His presence more than at any other time. When we allow His light and His love to shine through us, we will feel it within as well.

When you read the story of Hannah and her desperate prayers for a child, you will see the purpose of God unfold and His love to use her to bring forth a prophet! Will you allow Him to birth a "Samuel" in you? Will you persevere and trust Him? This book is about allowing God to take you through your trials to discover your purpose in Christ and more of His love in the process. As you allow Him to lead you through the trial, just as Hannah did, new desires and passions for God's glory will be birthed in you. New life and joy abounding will overflow from within you! Trust Him through it and do not let go, do not give up. Victory is promised!

"Give, and it will be given to you: good measure, pressed down, shaken together, and running over will be put into your bosom. For with the same measure that you use, it will be measured back to you." (Luke 6:38)

Let Go and Let God

God in His faithfulness never changes.
His love is constant.
He doesn't move, we do.

If in His love our trials break us,
It is simply to mold and to change us.

Let go and let God.
He loves you and will not fail or forsake you.

The change will bring trust and faith
And in you love, peace, and joy it will produce.

Let go and let God.
His love is constant
His plan never fails, we do.

He is always faithful
His love is true.
If you let Him, he will move you.

Let go and let God!

1

❧

The Betrothal

We do not see any background information for Elkanah and Hannah, but from the passage of I Samuel 1:4, "But to Hannah he would give a double portion, for he loved Hannah," we can infer that they were in love, even in being married in Jewish customs. Jewish families stay within their clans, as found in Genesis 24:1-4: "Abraham was now very old, and the Lord had blessed him in every way. He said to the senior servant in his household, the one in charge of all that he had, 'Put your hand under my thigh. I want you to swear by the Lord, the God of heaven and the God of earth, that you will not get a wife for my son from the daughters of the Canaanites, among whom I am living, but will go to my country and my own relatives and get a wife for my son Isaac.'"

According to Jewish customs, they would marry within their own people. "When the Lord your God brings you into the land you are entering to possess and drives out before you many nations—the Hittites, Girgashites, Amorites, Canaanites, Perizzites, Hivites and Jebusites, seven nations larger and stronger than you—when the Lord your God has delivered them over to you and you have defeated them, then you must destroy them totally. Make no treaty with them and show them no mercy. Do not intermarry with them. Do not give your daughters to their sons or take their daughters for your sons, for they will turn your children away from following me to serve other gods, and the Lord's anger will burn against you and will quickly destroy you." (Deuteronomy 7:1-4) This was to keep them following God instead of the idols and gods of other nations and peoples. Our marriage here on earth is a symbol of the unity between us and our Lord and is meant to be a holy union. "For your Maker is your husband, The Lord of hosts is His name; and your Redeemer is the Holy One of Israel; He is called the God of the whole earth." (Isaiah 54:5) The couple was betrothed, called *erusin* or *kiddushin* (Wikipedia, Wikipedia-Betrothal, 2018).

The first stage is the arrangement, and the bride-to-be is asked if she will agree to it. "Then they said, 'Let's call the young woman and ask her about it.' So, they called Rebekah and asked her, 'Will you go with this man?' 'I will go,' she said." (Genesis 24:57-58) The bride's acceptance is symbolized in the Israelites' acceptance to follow God. "So, Moses went back and summoned the elders of the people and set before them all the words the Lord had commanded him to speak. The people all responded together, 'We will do everything the Lord has said.' So, Moses brought their answer back to the Lord." (Exodus 19:7-8) It also symbolizes our acceptance and belief in Jesus Christ: "Yet to all who did receive Him, to those who believed in His name, He gave the right to become children of God." (John 1:12)

The parents of the couples agreed and a bride price was paid, known as the *mohar*. It is usually paid by the father of the groom to the father of the bride. Gifts are usually given to the bride as well. "Laban and Bethuel answered, 'This is from the Lord; we can say nothing to you one way or the other. Here is Rebekah; take her and go, and let her become the wife of your master's son, as the Lord has directed.' When Abraham's servant heard what they said, he bowed down to the ground before the Lord. Then the servant brought out gold and silver jewelry and articles of clothing and gave them to Rebekah; he also gave costly gifts to her brother and to her mother." (Genesis 24:50-53)

The bride price that was paid for us is Jesus Christ and His death on the cross. "In your relationships with one another, have the same mindset as Christ Jesus: Who, being in very nature God, did not consider equality with God something to be used to His own advantage; rather, He made Himself nothing by taking the very nature of a servant, being made in human likeness. And being found in appearance as a man, He humbled Himself by becoming obedient to death—even death on a cross!" (Philippians 2:5-8) But the verse that shows it all, the pain and the love He went through on the cross for all of mankind, is found in Isaiah 53:

"Who has believed our message and to whom has the arm of the Lord been revealed? He grew up before Him like a tender shoot, and like a root out of dry ground. He had no beauty or majesty to attract us to Him, nothing in His appearance that we should desire Him. He was despised and rejected by mankind, a man of suffering, and familiar with pain. Like one from whom people hide their faces He was despised, and we held Him in low esteem. Surely, He took up our pain and bore our suffering, yet we considered Him punished by God, stricken by Him, and afflicted. But He was pierced for our transgressions, He was crushed for our iniquities; the punishment that brought us peace was on Him, and by His wounds, we are healed. We all, like sheep, have gone astray, each of us has turned to our own way; and the Lord has laid on Him the iniquity of us all. He was oppressed and afflicted, yet He did not open His mouth; He was led like a lamb to the slaughter, and as a sheep, before its shearers is silent, so He did not open His mouth. By oppression and judgment, He was taken away. Yet who of His generation protested? For He was cut off from the land of the living; for the transgression of my people He was punished. He was assigned a grave with the wicked, and with the rich in His death, though He had done no violence, nor was any deceit in His mouth. Yet it was the Lord's will to crush Him and cause Him to suffer, and though the Lord makes His life an offering for sin, He will see His offspring and prolong his days, and the will of the Lord will prosper in His hand. After He has suffered, He will see the light of life and be satisfied; by His knowledge, My righteous servant will justify many, and He will bear their iniquities. Therefore, I will give Him a portion among the great, and He will divide the spoils with the strong, because He poured out His life unto death, and was numbered with the transgressors. For He bore the sin of many and made intercession for the transgressors."

When two people come together to be united as one, it is a beautiful thing. When they are truly in love, you can see it in their eyes as it overflows from their hearts. Elkanah's love for Hannah represents God's love for us in that even before we reach our spiritual maturity or our purpose in Him, in His overwhelming love for us He still gives us a double portion! The double portion is first the indwelling at conversion; the moment you ask Jesus into your heart. "Because you are his sons, God sent the Spirit of his Son into our hearts, the Spirit who calls out, 'Abba, Father.'" (Galatians 4:6) The other portion is the baptism of the Holy Spirit. As we **"surrender,"** which is one of the different meanings of the word "closed" in the verse, "the Lord closed her womb" (I Samuel 1:5), and seek Him with our whole heart, and ask the Lord into our heart, He baptizes us with His Holy Spirit. "But you will receive power when the Holy Spirit comes on you, and you will be my witnesses in Jerusalem, and in all Judea and Samaria, and to the ends of the earth." (Acts 1:8) When you are baptized in the Holy Spirit, His Spirit comes on you and consumes you! How great is our God!

Courting, the betrothal period, is a time of delight and wonder; you are getting to know each other and finding out each other's likes and dislikes, dreams, and interests. I imagine it was not much different with Hannah and Elkanah. The betrothal, *erusin*, meaning "bound," also called *kiddushin*, ceremony was given, and Elkanah and Hannah were promised to each other; it was a joyous occasion. This was what we call the engagement period, but at the betrothal, Hannah and Elkanah were considered married. This is when we first commit to Jesus Christ. When we give our hearts to Him, we are truly new in Him. "Therefore, if any man is in Christ, he is a new creation: old things are passed away; behold, all things become new." (II Corinthians 5:17) At the betrothal *erusin* stage, in ancient times, there was usually about a year before the wedding – the *nisu'in* stage - takes place. This is the stage in which the wedding is completed, and consummation takes place. At the betrothal stage, the bride is sanctified, and kept apart – this is what is known as *kiddushin*. The *kiddushin* term is also used to reference both the *erusin* and the *nisu'in* stage. When completed, the two are set apart and bound together, sanctified in holiness unto God. This is like the command the Lord gives us when we enter a relationship with Him. We are to leave our past life of sin behind as well as the bad influences that were associated with it. "Therefore, come out from among them, and be you separate, says the Lord, and touch not the unclean thing; and I will receive you." (II Corinthians 6:17) During the ceremony, the formal agreement is made, but the contract, the *ketubah* (Wikipedia, Wikipedia-Ketubah, 2018), is written in a special ceremony just before the wedding. In ancient times the *ketubah* was done at the *erusin*. Since then it has changed and is signed and read in a separate ceremony right before the wedding. I will cover more on the ketubah in the wedding chapter. In the ceremony, there are two blessings done over wine. The ceremony opens with the blessing called *kiddush*, "Blessed art thou, Lord our God, King of the universe, Creator of the fruit of the vine." This one is done with kiddush cups, which are beautifully embellished.

The *kiddush* blessing is also recited at other celebrations and holidays. The Rabbi hands the cup to the groom, who takes a sip. Following the *kiddush* blessing is another one called the *Birkat erusin*.

Birkat Erusin Blessing
Praised be Thou, O Lord our God, King of the universe who has sanctified us with His commandments and has commanded us concerning illicit relations; and has prohibited us those who are merely betrothed but has permitted to us those lawfully married to us by chuppah and kiddushin. Blessed art thou God, who has sanctified His people Israel by chuppah and kiddushin.

I must admit, I love the beauty and love in the holiness of the ceremonies and the awe of God that we should all have in committing ourselves to our soon-to-be husband or wife. This is a symbol of our unity with Jesus Christ. Picture Elkanah and Hannah standing before the priest knowing they were committing their selves to each other. I can picture, given what is written in I Samuel 1 about Hannah, that she stood there in a shy manner with a look of true humility about her. The bride would also wear a veil, which is called *badekin* (Wikipedia, Wikipedia-Views on Jewish Weddings, 2018), which was lifted to take the wine blessing, and then put back down afterward. "Behold, you are fair, my love; behold, you are fair; you have doves' eyes behind your veil: your hair is like a flock of goats, going down from mount Gilead." (Song of Solomon 4:1) A ring is given, and the ceremony is completed. When the groom gives the bride the ring, he recites, "Behold, by this ring you are consecrated to me as my wife according to the laws of Moses and Israel." They are considered married at this point, although they do not live together until the *Nisu'in*.

The courtship began, and both got to know each other. Do you remember the times in your life when you were dating? I remember I could not wait to see my date. It was always fun and full of excitement as we began the process of getting to know each other. But with God, it is a little bit different. You may have begun to think of God, and if you did not go to church, the inspiration suddenly filled your heart. Maybe you were going through a dark period brought on by yourself or someone else and where, if seeking out God was not important before, now you really need Him.

That is sort of the way it was with me. I grew up a Catholic, but never really knew who Jesus was; I was not taught to read the Bible for myself, and in church, I read about Him. I never really knew Him, that did not come until some very dark years with my husband, a time in which the will to continue to live could only come with God's help. I called out to Him, and He saved me. God "courts" us, so to speak, by giving us signs, convicting our hearts while we are living in sin, or, before we are saved by the blood of Jesus. "And when He has come, He will convict the world of sin, and of righteousness, and of judgment." (John 16:8)

Eventually, the sin you are living in will catch up to you if you do not respond to God's leading as He begins to draw you to Himself. "No one can come to me unless the Father who sent me draws them, and I will raise them up at the last day." (John 6:44) The people God puts in your path to witness, the times you are around someone listening to praise music, or talking about their faith or the Sunday sermon, and many other ways, are all the many different avenues God will use to lead you, to draw you to Himself to receive Jesus as your Savior. If you do not heed the call, your sin will catch up to you, and you will reap what you sow. "Do not be deceived, God is not mocked; for whatever a man sows, that he will also reap. For he who sows to his flesh will of the flesh reap corruption, but he who sows to the Spirit will of the Spirit reap everlasting life." (Galatians 6:7-8) Satan may mean these things for your destruction, but God allows them to get your attention and cause you to think about your actions, your soul, and where you will spend eternity. "Behold, God works all these things, twice, in fact, three times with a man, to bring back his soul from the Pit, that he may be enlightened with the light of life." (Job 33:29-30)

Once He has your attention and you realize you need a change in your heart and spirit, the Holy Spirit will convict your heart and lead you in the way you should pray. He will also place people in your path to help lead you the rest of the way. "Then Jesus came to them and said, 'All authority in heaven and on earth has been given to me. Therefore, go and make disciples of all nations, baptizing them in the name of the Father and of the Son and of the Holy Spirit, and teaching them to obey everything I have commanded you. And surely, I am with you always, to the very end of the age.'" (Matthew 28:18-20)

These harvest workers, disciples of God, will lead you and help you to pray to receive our Lord. "Yet to all who did receive Him, to those who believed in His name, he gave the right to become children of God." (John 1:12) It is your faith, your belief in Him, and your confession that you receive His Holy Spirit and are saved. "If you declare with your mouth, 'Jesus is Lord,' and believe in your heart that God raised him from the dead, you will be saved. For it is with your heart that you believe and are justified, and it is with your mouth that you profess your faith and are saved." (Romans 10:9-10)

God allows some trials to teach you, convict you, or draw something out of you. "In this, you greatly rejoice, though now for a little while, if need be, you have been grieved by various trials, that the genuineness of your faith, being much more precious than gold that perishes, though it is tested by fire, may be found to praise, honor, and glory at the revelation of Jesus Christ, whom having not seen you love. Though now you do not see Him, yet believing, you rejoice with joy inexpressible and full of glory, receiving the end of your faith—the salvation of your souls." (I Peter 1:6-9)

There are seasons for everything, even trials. (Ecclesiastes 3:1) "There is a time for everything and a season for every activity under the heavens." So, there must have been a purpose for Hannah to go through this painful trial of being barren, a trial that would draw something out of her and one that would bear much fruit, and in the process bring her great joy. There will be fruit harvested from your trial as well! It is promised! (Psalm 1:3) "That person is like a tree planted by streams of water, which yields its fruit in season and whose leaf does not wither-- whatever they do prospers."

The fruit she would bear would bring much glory to God, and we were all created for His glory. (Isaiah 43:6-7) "I will say to the north, 'Give them up!' and to the south, 'Do not hold them back!' Bring My sons from afar, and My daughters from the ends of the earth—everyone who is called by my name, whom I created for my glory, whom I formed and made."

You may be asking, what did Hannah do to warrant a closed womb? I asked the same thing. Again, sometimes our trials are due to someone else's bad choices, and maybe we get wrapped up in those choices, finding ourselves doing something we would not ordinarily do. This was probably the case with Hannah. Marriage is to be between one man and one woman, so polygamy might have been the reason. Jewish people used to marry more than one wife, but it was never intended to be that way. Our marriage here on earth is a symbol of our relationship with our Lord. We are to have only one God, one Savior, Jesus Christ. "For even if there are so-called gods, whether in heaven or on earth (as there are many gods and many lords), yet for us there is one God, the Father, of whom are all things, and we for Him; and one Lord Jesus Christ, through whom are all things, and through whom we live." (I Corinthians 8:5-6)

In the beginning, when God created man and woman, He called the man to be joined to his wife (singular), not wives (plural). "Therefore, a man shall leave his father and mother and be joined to his wife, and they shall become one flesh." (Genesis 2:24)

God closed Hannah's womb, and the Bible never really said exactly why or if Elkanah ever thought of the reason, but God did use the situation for a purpose. You might also ask, why Hannah and not Peninnah? To be used of God you must have a humble heart. "God opposes the proud but gives grace to the humble." (James 4:6) You can clearly see in I Samuel 1:6 that Peninnah was mean-spirited: "And her rival also provoked her severely, to make her miserable, because the Lord had closed her womb.". Teasing Hannah about not having children does not seem very humble. The name Hannah comes from the Hebrew word *Channah*, meaning favor or grace. That kind of explains it, doesn't it? Hannah did not retaliate but wept. This also shows that she has a sensitive and humble heart.

Hannah may have had to endure a season of barrenness, but good would come of it! The Betrothal is a period of preparation as trials prepare us for the next step of God's purpose for us. If you keep going, you will make it to the purpose God has for you. He will also use you along the way to be a blessing to others.

"Unto the upright, there arises light in the darkness; He is gracious and full of compassion, and righteous." (Psalm 112:4)

2

∽

Wedding Day!

Finally, the wedding day is almost here! Among all the traditional Jewish wedding rituals and ceremonies, I imagine that the wedding day, *Nisu'in*, which means "marriage," was the day they looked forward to the most. This is the day that the couple finalized the wedding and could live together as husband and wife. Imagine Elkanah and Hannah, deeply in love and brimming over with excitement as the day neared and they joined together in spirit and in heart as man and wife.

The Erusin ceremony is completed, and closer to the wedding, there is an *Aufruf* ceremony, meaning "calling up." This is where the groom (or the couple) recites a blessing over the Torah and is showered with candy. Before the Aufruf ceremony, the bride makes a gift of a new tallit, (Wikipedia, Wikipedia--Tallit, 2018) which is a fringed garment. It has special twined and knotted fringes, known as *tzitzit,* attached to the four corners. The cloth part is known as the *beged*, meaning "garment." It is usually made from wool or cotton. This garment is a prayer shawl and worn over the groom's head. The bride making a new *tallit* symbolizes the formation of a new shared Jewish household.

The beauty and holiness of these ceremonies are awe-inspiring due to the symbolism regarding our Lord and Savior. The Church is the bride of Christ. "For Zion's sake, I will not keep silent, for Jerusalem's sake, I will not remain quiet, till her vindication shines out like the dawn, her salvation like a blazing torch. The nations will see your vindication, and all kings your glory; you will be called by a new name that the mouth of the Lord will bestow. You will be a crown of splendor in the Lord's hand, a royal diadem in the hand of your God. No longer will they call you Deserted or name your land Desolate. But you will be called Hephzibah, and your land Beulah; for the Lord will take delight in you, and your land will be married. As a young man marries a young woman, so will your Builder marry you; as a bridegroom rejoices over his bride, so will your God rejoice over you." (Isaiah 62:1-5) The representation of being "The bride of Christ" is the unity and oneness that will take place both once saved and when we reach our heavenly home. There will be no more sin, no more heartache, and no more illness in heaven because the evil one, Satan, will be thrown into his eternal home. There will be no evil in heaven!

As the wedding day for the Church approaches, the day the Church arises and becomes the Church of Christ as God always intended us to be, there will be a "calling up," which we call the rapture. The word "rapture," according to Webster's New American Dictionary, means "the state of being carried away with joy, love, etc.; ecstasy." (Webster, 1995). Doesn't that seem a lot like "calling up?"

"But you, brothers and sisters, are not in darkness so that this day should surprise you like a thief. You are all children of the light and children of the day. We do not belong to the night or to the darkness. So then, let us not be like others, who are asleep, but let us be awake and sober. For those who sleep, sleep at night, and those who get drunk, get drunk at night. But since we belong to the day, let us be sober, putting on faith and love as a breastplate, and the hope of salvation as a helmet. For God did not appoint us to suffer wrath but to receive salvation through our Lord Jesus Christ. He died for us so that, whether we are awake or asleep, we may live together with Him." (I Thessalonians 5:4-10)

And in another verse in the Old Testament, our being called up is written even more clearly: "But your dead will live; their bodies will rise. You who dwell in the dust, wake up and shout for joy. Your dew is like the dew of the morning; the earth will give birth to her dead. Go, my people, enter your rooms and shut the doors behind you; hide yourselves for a little while until His wrath has passed by. See, the Lord is coming out of His dwelling to punish the people of the earth for their sins. The earth will disclose the bloodshed upon her; she will conceal her slain no longer." (Isaiah 26:19-21)

The bride will also prepare herself spiritually; that is what we, the Church, are to be doing as well. That is what our life here on earth is – preparation for where we will spend eternity. Have you thought of it? Are you prepared?

The bride prepares herself by completing the Bridal Mikvah. (Berry, 2018)This has to be done no more than four days before the actual wedding. This is a cleansing, and the bride must not be on her period. There is a Mikvah pool in which this takes place; this is the "baptism of the bride" and is symbolic of the Lord commanding Moses to have the people consecrate themselves to Him. "And the Lord said to Moses, "Go to the people and consecrate them today and tomorrow. Have them wash their clothes and be ready by the **third day,** because on that day the Lord will come down on Mount Sinai in the sight of all the people." (Exodus 19:10-11)

We are cleansed of our sins by the blood of Jesus Christ. "But when the kindness and love of God our Savior appeared, He saved us, not because of righteous things we had done, but because of his mercy. He saved us through the washing of rebirth and renewal by the Holy Spirit, whom he poured out on us generously through Jesus Christ our Savior, so that, having been justified by His grace, we might become heirs having the hope of eternal life." (Titus 3:4-7) Jesus died, was buried, and on the **third day**, He rose to glory! "And he said, "The Son of Man must suffer many things and be rejected by the elders, the chief priests and the teachers of the law, and he must be killed and on the **third day** be raised to life." (Luke 9:22)

A Mikvah is not only a source of purification, but also a tradition of being reborn. Entering the Mikvah is an act of letting go of the self, and when one exists, the Mikvah is an act of rebirth. This symbolizes how we are "born again" when we receive Jesus Christ.

"Now there was a Pharisee, a man named Nicodemus who was a member of the Jewish ruling council. He came to Jesus at night and said, 'Rabbi, we know that you are a teacher who has come from God. For no one could perform the signs you are doing if God were not with him.' Jesus replied, 'Very truly I tell you, no one can see the kingdom of God unless they are born again.' 'How can someone be born when they are old?' Nicodemus asked. 'Surely they cannot enter a second time into their mother's womb to be born!' Jesus answered, 'Very truly I tell you, no one can enter the kingdom of God unless they are born of water and the Spirit. Flesh gives birth to flesh, but the Spirit gives birth to spirit. You should not be surprised at my saying, 'You must be born again.' The wind blows wherever it pleases. You hear its sound, but you cannot tell where it comes from or where it is going. So, it is with everyone born of the Spirit.'" (John 3:1-8)

Many couples like to celebrate this commitment to each other after both having taken part in their own individual Mikvah. The bride and the groom have a chance for individual reflection, thought, and rebirth before joining together to become one. I am sure during this time Elkanah and Hannah had much to reflect on; they were about to become husband and wife. This would be a new life from their current one with new adventures together, and especially the best adventure of all: having a family!

Noah and the Ark is symbolic of being baptized into Christ. The earth at that time was rampant with sin, and God found Noah righteous and spared him and his family. This is where we also are baptized when we receive Jesus as Lord and Savior. " In the ark, a few people, only eight souls, were saved through water. And this water symbolizes baptism that now saves you also--not the removal of dirt from the body but the pledge of a clear conscience toward God. It saves you by the resurrection of Jesus Christ." (I Peter 3:20-21) Baptism is an outward showing of what the blood of Christ does for our soul; it cleanses us and saves us. When we ask and receive Him into our hearts, we are saved and born again, baptized into the family of God! "Or don't you know that all of us who were baptized into Christ Jesus were baptized into his death? We were therefore buried with Him through baptism into death so that, just as Christ was raised from the dead through the glory of the Father, we too may live a new life. For if we have been united with him in a death like his, we will certainly also be united with him in a resurrection like his. For we know that our old self was crucified with him so that the body ruled by sin might be done away with, that we should no longer be slaves to sin—because anyone who has died has been set free from sin. Now if we died with Christ, we believe that we will also live with him. For we know that since Christ was raised from the dead, he cannot die again; death no longer has mastery over him. The death he died, he died to sin once for all; but the life he lives, he lives to God. In the same way, count yourselves dead to sin but alive to God in Christ Jesus." (Romans 6:3-11)

The day is nearing closer and closer, the bride has made herself ready, and all the planning and the previous ceremonies have been one celebration after another. And yet, Hannah probably was a little apprehensive. After all, she was a virgin and had never been with a man, and for a woman of humble character, as Hannah seemed to be, it must have been a little scary. Not only that, she had been under her parents' roof all these years; it would be a big change and a whole new life. That was exactly the way I felt: scared and exhilarated at the same time! When you received Jesus for the first time, weren't you just as overjoyed? At the same time, you were not quite sure what to expect. The old life of sin was gone and a new one awaited. Hannah must have felt this same way, and I am sure she must have had many one-on-one talks with her mother.

As said in the previous chapter, the *ketubah*, or marriage contract, used to be written and signed at the *Erusin* ceremony. Now it is done right before the *nisu'in*, the wedding. It is called the Tenaim Ceremony. Tenaim means "conditions," and that is what the *ketubah* is; the conditions for the protection of the bride and what the groom is prepared to do for her in the marriage and in case of divorce. It also includes the bride price, the *mohar*. It is like the covenant God makes with all His people, with us personally. "In that day,' declares the Lord, 'you will call me 'my husband'; you will no longer call me 'my master.' I will remove the names of the Baals from her lips; no longer will their names be invoked. In that day I will make a covenant for them with the beasts of the field, the birds in the sky, and the creatures that move along the ground. Bow and sword and battle I will abolish from the land, so that all may lie down in safety. I will betroth you to me forever; I will betroth you in righteousness and justice, in love and compassion. I will betroth you in faithfulness, and you will acknowledge the Lord.'" (Hosea 2:16-20) The *ketubah* is written and signed in front of two witnesses. This is considered a holy union, and breaking this covenant would have serious consequences, which is reminiscent of God's initial covenant with Israel: "Then Moses went up to God, and the Lord called to him from the mountain and said, 'This is what you are to say to the descendants of Jacob and what you are to tell the people of Israel: 'You yourselves have seen what I did to Egypt, and how I carried you on eagles' wings and brought you to myself. Now if you obey me fully and keep my covenant, then out of all nations you will be my treasured possession. Although the whole earth is mine, you will be for me a kingdom of priests and a holy nation.' These are the words you are to speak to the Israelites.'" (Exodus 19:3-6)

The contract is read, a plate is broken, and the ceremony is completed. The breaking of the plate symbolizes that breaking the engagement is final and not easily mended. (Berry, 2018) One more step completed and one more to go before the *nisu'in*. Hannah and Elkanah would soon be married, living together under one roof. Excitement fills their hearts more and more as the final stage draws near!

The wedding ceremony under Jewish customs cannot take place on days they consider holy to God, which are the Sabbath, the holy days of Rosh Hashanah, Yom Kippur, Passover, Shavuot, and the first and last days of Sukkot, and around certain fasting days.

The ceremony itself is held under a Chuppah (pronounced Huppah). It means, "canopy," "covering" or "protection," and the linen should be white, which stands for purity. "Let us rejoice and celebrate and give Him the glory. For the marriage of the Lamb has come, and His bride has made herself ready. Fine linen, bright and clean, was given to her to wear. (Fine linen stands for the righteous acts of God's holy people.)" (Revelation 19:7-8) Wedded under a canopy, the covering stands for yet more: now the two will be under one roof, they will be one, building a home together. It is also symbolic of our protection under the shed blood of Jesus Christ. "Grace and peace to you from him who is, and who was, and who is to come, and from the seven spirits before his throne, and from Jesus Christ, who is the faithful witness, the firstborn from the dead, and the ruler of the kings of the earth. To Him who loves us and has freed us from our sins by his blood, and has made us to be a kingdom and priests to serve His God and Father—to Him be glory and power forever and ever! Amen." (Revelation 1:4-6)

Traditionally the ceremony is also done outside. (Center, Chabad.org--wedding ceremony, 1993-2018) The chuppah is open on all sides as a reminder of Abraham and Sarah; they had their tent open on all sides to welcome people in unconditionally. Another reason is that having it outside under the stars is reminiscent of the blessing God gave to Abraham. "Then the word of the Lord came to him, saying, 'This one will not be your heir, but one who comes from your own body will be your heir.' He took him outside and said, 'Look up at the sky and count the stars--if indeed you can count them.' Then he said to him, 'So shall your offspring be.'" (Genesis 15:4-5)

Right before the procession, after the Tenaim Ceremony, there is a Bedeken Ceremony. (Wikipedia, Wikipedia, 2018) This is when the groom covers the bride with a veil and at the end lifts it – and this time stays lifted—just like when the veil of the temple was torn when Jesus died. "But now in Christ Jesus, you who once were far away have been brought near by the blood of Christ. For He Himself is our peace, who has made the two one and has torn down the dividing wall of hostility." (Ephesians 2:13-14) Jesus, by His death on the cross, tore the dividing wall so that now we can approach God. "But Jesus let out a loud cry and breathed His last. The curtain of the temple was torn in two from top to bottom." (Mark 15:37-38) We can go to God in prayer through His name. "Truly, truly, I tell you, whoever believes in Me will also do the works that I am doing. He will do even greater things than these because

I am going to the Father. And I will do whatever you ask in my name, so that the Father may be glorified in the Son. If you ask Me anything in My name, I will do it." (Mark 14:12-14)

Jewish people also veil the bride as a reminder of how Jacob was tricked into marrying Leah before Rachel. I can see Hannah as she stands before Elkanah, both looking at each other. He is about to veil her face, and their eyes meet, and there is a look of love in their eyes.

At last the final stages of the wedding ceremony are here, and as each parent escorts the bride and groom to the chuppah, there is music playing. Their families and guests are waiting for their arrival. There are also candles symbolic of the flickering light and fire that occurred at the time the Torah was given at Mount Sinai between God and Israel. The candles are also meant to wish the couple a new life together filled with light and joy. Picture Hannah who was probably a little bit nervous about finalizing all the events in the ceremonies and now she is actually being escorted to the final wedding ceremony. I can imagine the look of pure joy and beauty that exuberates a glow about her, just like Moses glowed when he was in the presence of God. "But whenever Moses went in before the Lord to speak with Him, he would remove the veil until he came out. And when he came out, he would tell the Israelites what he had been commanded, they saw that his face was radiant. Then Moses would put the veil back over his face until he went in to speak with the Lord." (Exodus 34:34-35)

The final stage of our wedding as the bride of Christ is when we are called up to heaven at the last trumpet call. "Listen, I tell you a mystery: We will not all sleep, but we will all be changed—in a flash, in the twinkling of an eye, at the last trumpet. For the trumpet will sound, the dead will be raised imperishable, and we will be changed. For the perishable must clothe itself with the imperishable, and the mortal with immortality. When the perishable has been clothed with the imperishable and the mortal with immortality, then the saying that is written will come to pass: "Death has been swallowed up in victory." (I Corinthians 15:51-54)

The groom is escorted to the chuppah first and is welcomed by the Rabbi. (Center, Chabad.org--wedding ceremony, 1993-2018) The groom arriving first is symbolic of Jesus being the firstborn to be raised from the dead. "The Son is the image of the invisible God, the firstborn over all creation. For in him, all things were created: things in heaven and on earth, visible and invisible, whether thrones or powers or rulers or authorities; all things have been created through Him and for Him. He is before all things, and in Him all things hold together. And He is the head of the body, the church; He is the beginning and the firstborn from among the dead, so that in everything He might have the supremacy. For God was pleased to have all His fullness dwell in Him, and through Him to reconcile to Himself all things, whether things on earth or things in heaven, by making peace through his blood, shed on the cross." (Colossians 1:15-20)

Then the bride is escorted to the chuppah and is welcomed, and she circles the groom seven times. This is symbolic of the Israelites encircling Jericho seven times breaking down the walls around Jericho, representing now all barriers between the couple are broken and now the bride is one with her husband. "How long will you wander, O faithless daughter? For the Lord has created a new thing in the land—A woman will surround a man." (Jeremiah 31:22)

After both the bride and the groom are welcomed under the chuppah, a prayer is said by the Rabbi asking God to bless the couple. Then the *Sheva Brachot*, which means, "The seven blessings," is recited by the Rabbi over a cup of wine. Before each blessing, the Rabbi announces the couple as "honored with recitation of the _____blessing." At the end of each blessing, the couple takes a sip of wine. The first blessing is the blessing of the wine and the other six are of a marriage theme and include a special blessing for newlyweds.

The Seven Blessings (Wikipedia, Wikipedia-Sheva Brachot, 2018) (Center, Chabad.org-7 blessings, 1993-2018)

1. *Praised are You, O Lord our God, King of the Universe, Creator of the fruit of the vine.*
2. *Praised are You, O Lord our God, King of the Universe, who created all things for Your glory.*
3. *Praised are You, O Lord our God, King of the Universe, Creator of man.*
4. *Praised are You, O Lord our God, King of the Universe, who created man and woman in Your image, fashioning woman from man as his mate, that together they might perpetuate life. Praised are You, O Lord, Creator of man.*
5. *May Zion rejoice as her children are restored to her in joy. Praised are You, O Lord, who causes Zion to rejoice at her children's return.*
6. *Grant perfect joy to these loving companions, as You did to the first man and woman in the Garden of Eden. Praised are You, O Lord, who grants the joy of bride and groom.*
7. *Praised are You, O Lord our God, King of the Universe, who created joy and gladness, bride and groom, mirth, song, delight and rejoicing, love and harmony, peace and companionship. O Lord our God may there ever be heard in the cities of Judah and in the streets of Jerusalem voices of joy and gladness, voices of bride and groom, the jubilant voices of those joined in marriage under the bridal canopy, the voices of young people feasting and singing. Praised are You, O Lord, who causes the groom to rejoice with his bride.*

The couple finalizes the wedding ceremony with the bride and groom shattering a glass wrapped in cloth. It is symbolic of the destruction of the Temple and serves as a reminder that life and marriage are fragile, and the couple should enjoy every moment. The wedding ritual ends with the newly married couple spending time alone in *Yihud*, in private. There are two stages in a Jewish wedding, the Betrothal stage and the

Consummation stage. This is the final stage of the consummation stage, the *nisu'in* being the first part, and is representative of the Holy Spirit filling us when we ask the Lord into our hearts.

"Because you are his sons, God sent the Spirit of his Son into our hearts, the Spirit who calls out, 'Abba, Father.'" (Galatians 4:6)

Once all the rituals and ceremonies are complete the newlyweds, family, and guests enjoy a feast accompanied by more music. And of course, you cannot read about a wedding feast without thinking about the wedding feast of the saints!

"Then the angel said to me, 'Write this: Blessed are those who are invited to the wedding supper of the Lamb!' And he added, 'These are the true words of God.'" (Revelation 19:9)

3

Love Grows

It has been a whirlwind of excitement! There has been one ceremony after another and then the wedding feast with both families and friends all gathered together to celebrate the union of the bride and groom. The newlyweds are filled with excitement and wonder as they begin their first week together as husband and wife. In the Jewish faith, the celebration continues through the first week, called The Sheva Brachot Week. (Center, Chabad.org-- newlyweds, 1993-2018) The week of festivities is a series of small celebrations held to honor the couple. The meal traditionally includes singing some of the words of the Torah. Before the Grace after Meals – blessings and thanksgiving after a meal –two full cups of wine are prepared. One cup is for the one who leads the Grace after Meals, and the other is for the Sheva Brachot blessings. The one who leads the Grace adds some words such as, "God in whose abode there is joy, of whose bounty we have eaten." All those who are present will respond in a like manner. There must be present ten adult men present to recite the Sheva Brachot. The seven blessings are recited after the meal and consist of requests for God to bless the new couple. After the six blessings are recited, the person who led the Grace after Meals recites the wine blessing. The wine in the two cups is blended and the bride sips from one cup and the groom takes a sip from the other. They get the royal treatment and are accompanied by an "honor guard" wherever they go.

It is also customary for the groom to do an *Aliyah*, which is the honor of reciting one of the blessings over the Torah on the Shabbat, which is the Sabbath after the wedding. Under certain circumstances, the bride and groom may be exempt from fasting during their first week of marriage, but it is the Rabbi who makes this decision. Also, when the groom goes to pray at the synagogue, the whole congregation omits the Tachanum, which is a penitential prayer. These are omitted on festival days in honor of the festive atmosphere. With all the continued festivities of the week, I can picture Hannah and Elkanah with an air of delight and pure joy about them.

As the days set in it will also be a time of truly getting to know one another. It is one thing to see each other from day to day, but quite another to live with them. That is when you truly get to know someone – when you are with them day and night. You get to know all their likes and dislikes, all their habits and odd quirks. After the week of festivities is over, the couple will need time to be alone and get adjusted to being married and living together and get calmed down from the adrenaline of all the excitement. This is when it will hit: "I am married!"

It is a Jewish custom based on the Bible for newly married men to abstain from battle and to remain home and free from traveling separately for one year. "When a man takes a new wife, he shall not go out in the army, nor shall it obligate him for any matter. He shall remain free for his home for one year and delight his wife whom he has taken" (Deuteronomy 24:5) A marriage built on a strong foundation will last, and taking time to nurture your new relationship as husband and wife is an important part of that.

Nurturing your new relationship in Christ is just as important! "Therefore, I urge you, brothers and sisters, in view of God's mercy, to offer your bodies as a living sacrifice, holy and pleasing to God—this is your true and proper worship. Do not conform to the pattern of this world but be transformed by the renewing of your mind. Then you will be able to test and approve what God's will is—His good, pleasing, and perfect will." (Romans 12:1-2) We live in a fallen world, a world in which our enemy the devil roams around looking for easy prey! "Be sober, be vigilant; because your adversary the devil, as a roaring lion, walks about, seeking whom he may devour." (I Peter 5:8) How can you in your natural self defeat a supernatural enemy? You cannot! "I am the vine, you are the branches: He that abides in me, and I in him, the same brings forth much fruit: for without me you can do nothing." (John 15:5) You need Jesus, you need the power and strength of His Holy Spirit within to live victoriously. "These things I have spoken unto you, that in me you might have peace. In the world you shall have tribulation: but be of good cheer; I have overcome the world." (John 16:33) You would not eat once a week or on special holidays; your body would get sick. It is the same with our spirit; you need your spiritual food as well. "And Jesus said unto them, I am the bread of life: he that comes to me shall never hunger, and he that believes on me shall never thirst." (John 6:35)

The time alone will help Hannah and Elkanah to get to know one another even more intimately. You get to know one another on a much deeper level living together, and the more time you spend with each other, the deeper your relationship will be. This is the same with your spiritual relationship. The more time you spend with the Lord, talking to Him as you would a friend, praying, and also taking the time to listen as well, and read the Bible will help you to deepen your relationship with Him.

After all the wedding celebrations are finally finished, Hannah and Elkanah begin their day-to-day living activities as a couple. Living with someone and seeing not only their "dating" face, their best face, but their happy face, their sad face, and even their angry face is when you truly get to know them and helps build a strong marriage foundation. Living day-to-day and seeing all sides of someone helps to deepen the relationship. You see it and you do not care, you love them anyway. That is what God did for us:

"But God commends his love toward us, in that, while we were yet sinners, Christ died for us." (Romans 5:8)

Mankind was sinning against Him, they beat Him beyond human recognition, hung Him on a cross and He did it all for love. He did it anyway. That is love!

"We love because He first loved us." (I John 4:19)
"In this is love, not that we loved God, but that he loved us, and sent his Son to be the propitiation for our sins." (I John 4:10)

Hannah and Elkanah, like in any new relationship, need this quality time together to grow their love even more. This will help them get through problems together when they arise. A house needs a strong foundation first before the rest is built. It needs the foundation to be strong to hold a well-built house, or it will not be able to withstand the winds of trouble. "He is like a man who built a house, and dug deep, and laid the foundation on a rock: and when the flood arose, the stream beat vehemently upon that house, and could not shake it: for it was founded upon a rock." (Luke 6:48)

When you were first saved, and everything was new, you dove into reading the Word of God, going to church, spending time with God, and getting to know Him. You were not instantly thrown into battle. Knowing the Word of God, which is your weapon, helps you to know each piece of weaponry found in the Word to use for each situation that arises. "For the word of God is living, and powerful, and sharper than any two-edged sword, piercing even to the dividing asunder of soul and spirit, and of the joints and marrow, and is a discerner of the thoughts and intents of the heart." (Hebrews 4:12) That is why it is so important to read and study the Bible for yourself and not just wait until Sunday. God wants to reveal things to you on a personal level and this is done through your own study time. "Till I come, give attendance to reading, to exhortation, to doctrine." (I Timothy 4:13)

In reading about David and Goliath, I found it interesting that instead of saying, "Your armor does not fit me," when he was about to go up against Goliath, David reasoned: "And David girded his sword upon his armor, and he attempted to go; for he had not tried it. And David said unto Saul, I cannot go with these; for I have not tried them. And David put them off him." (I Samuel 17:39) The word "tried" here means, "to test," or "to prove." This means you cannot use something that you have not tried out first in order to know it. How can God remind you of Scripture when you need it if you have not read it first? "But the Comforter, who is the Holy Spirit, whom the Father will send in my name, he shall teach you all things, and bring all things to your remembrance, whatsoever I have said unto you." (John 14:26)

From I Samuel 1:4, "But to Hannah he would give a double portion, for he loved Hannah," we know that they took time to spend together as specified in Deuteronomy 24:5, that Elkanah should not travel and go into battle, but spend time at home. It does not mean he does not have to work, but only that he should limit his traveling and being away from home during the first year. They took time to get to know each other as a married couple and build their foundation together. This is why it is said, "he loved Hannah." They took the time to let their love grow for each other.

As part of allowing their love to grow, Hannah and Elkanah had to assume new roles. Before, Hannah was a daughter living with her parents and had duties to fulfill in her daily life as a daughter obeying her parents. Elkanah, likewise, was a son living with his parents and had his duties as a son. Now, they are in their own household and have new roles to assume as husband and wife, and learning and growing into those roles will also assist in growing their love, their relationship, and their marriage into a firm and solid foundation. As the husband, it was Elkanah's duty to provide the home and to take care of his family, and it was Hannah's duty as his wife to take care of the home. What once was an "I" decision now becomes a "we" decision. Things have changed, and now they have to make decisions based on the two of them.

To allow your spiritual relationship in Christ to grow, the once "I," and "all about me" syndrome has to change as well. For your relationship in Christ to grow, He must come first. "He must increase, but I must decrease." (John 3:30) When we put God first, His love flows freely through us, it is a love exchange. We receive His love, and in return that love helps us to not only love Him but to love others and ourselves as well. "Love the Lord your God with all your heart and with all your soul and with all your strength and with all your mind'; and, 'Love your neighbor as yourself.'" (Luke 10:27) As you seek Him first, you will not want to do anything that displeases Him, including hurting others or even yourself. As a child of God, you are not just thinking about yourself; you put Him first, and this brings you peace and joy. You are blessed! It is a win-win situation!

We use that same principle in marriage. When you put your spouse's needs before your own, there is peace and less strife, and your marriage will grow. This is marital harmony and in Jewish culture is known as "shalom bayit," and it is valued in Jewish tradition. The Talmud, which is the primary source of Jewish religious laws and theology, states that the husband should love his wife as much as he loves himself and honor her more than himself as well. (Wikipedia, Wikipedia--views on Jewish marriage, 2018)With both of you doing the same, you both win and your love grows!

Being united in Christ, just as it was Elkanah's duty to provide, your heavenly Father knows your needs, and as long as you keep putting Him first, seeking Him and His will, He will provide for you, He will lead you, and give you the wisdom and help needed for each situation. As He provides, your faith will grow, and your love for Him will grow deeper and stronger. The intimate relationship you desire to have with the Lord will become rooted in your spirit, and you will become immovable.

"But seek ye first the kingdom of God, and His righteousness; and all these things shall be added unto you." (Matthew 6:33)

4

∽

Family!

Family: when most people get married, they want to have children. This was something especially desired and expected in the Jewish family tradition and is taken from Genesis 1:28: "God blessed them and said to them, "Be fruitful and increase in number; fill the earth and subdue it. Rule over the fish in the sea and the birds in the sky and over every living creature that moves on the ground." Having children was important to carry on the family name.

In your Christian faith, as you grow and learn the Word of God, your passion and zeal for God and His heart grow within you as well. You are birthed with new desires to do something for God, to serve Him. Passions for the purpose God has for you are coming alive in you. Much like the desire to have children. But roadblocks continually seem to be popping up. This can mean different things; some sins you still need to repent and deal with, or maybe something else you still need to learn. Maybe some connections are a part of your purpose you have not made, but regardless, you feel stunted! You are frustrated, confused, and full of despair! Not a good feeling, especially when God has not revealed the "why" behind the roadblocks.

This must have been the way Hannah felt. She and Elkanah had been growing closer and closer, they were more in love than ever and their marriage seemed firm. So, they decided to have children, but year after year passed, and still nothing.

God wants you to have children just as He wants you to fulfill the purpose He has for you. "The Lord Almighty has sworn, "Surely, as I have planned, so it will be, and as I have purposed, so it will happen." (Isaiah 14:24) God has a purpose for each one of us but He wants us to be ready for it before we begin to operate in it. There may still be some more parts to the puzzle so to speak, that He needs to reveal, more you need to learn, or more areas that you need to grow spiritually before He allows you to move in your purpose. "We have much to say about this, but it is hard to make it clear to you because you no longer try to understand. Though by this time you ought to be teachers, you need someone to teach you the elementary truths of God's word all over again. You need milk, not solid food! Anyone who lives on milk, being still an infant, is not acquainted with the teaching about righteousness. But solid food is for the mature, who by constant use have trained themselves to distinguish good from evil." (Hebrews 5:11-14) God does not want you to begin moving in your purpose and then fall. This will happen if you are truly not ready to handle it. As with any new move in position, a promotion in Christ will also come with new trials to face. Only God, who knows the end from the beginning, knows whether you are ready to handle it. So, sometimes the delays are for your protection. "Remember the former things, those of long ago; I am God, and there is no other; I am God, and there is none like Me. I make known the end from the beginning, from ancient times, what is still to come. I say, 'My purpose will stand, and I will do all that I please." (Isaiah 46:10)

In the case of Hannah and Elkanah, they were probably filled with excitement at the thought of starting their family, and then as year after year went by and there were still no children, discouragement and confusion probably set in. God had another purpose for her barrenness. When the trials get difficult, that is when we have to remember the cross and the pain He endured on our behalf and tell ourselves, "If He would go through all of that for me, then this trial, and the length and severity of it, must be for a good reason. This too shall pass and turn out for my good."

"And we know that in all things God works for the good of those who love Him, who have been called according to His purpose." (Romans 8:28) God did have a good reason for Hannah's barrenness, and He had a good reason for your delays. Trust Him. "Trust in the Lord with all your heart and lean not on your own understanding; in all your ways submit to Him, and He will make your paths straight." (Proverbs 3:5-6)

What dreams and desires has the Lord placed in your heart? Has it seemed as if it is taking forever to manifest? Look back at the past few years since that passion was born in you. What changes have taken place in you since? We are growing in our faith and the knowledge of the Word, and we think that we have matured, then out of the blue another trial hits and we find that there is still more we need to be weeded out of our hearts and more we need to learn. Trust in the process. If God birthed the dream in you to start with, He will certainly bring it to fruition. "Being confident of this very thing, that he who has begun a good work in you will perform it until the day of Jesus Christ." (Philippians 1:6) He knows your heart better than you do! Trust in that same love that died for you and saved you to also see you through every trial, every step of your growth process, every step of your purpose, and into eternity. "If we had forgotten the name of our God or spread out our hands to a foreign god, would not God have discovered it since he knows the secrets of the heart?" (Psalm 44:20-21)

Year after year Elkanah traveled to Shiloh to worship from their home in Ramanthaim Zophim. This was a 12-mile trip and no easy task. He had camels, two wives, and children. Today some people cannot walk even a mile, and how much more difficult to do it in the hot sun. Elkanah was devoted to the Lord, and yet still had no children. It did not stop him or change his devotion to the Lord. He continued to make the trip year after year even though Hannah, the one he loved and gave a double portion to, remained childless. Our devotion to the Lord should be as such: devotion to Him and not to what He gives us. Having children was important and it did not alter Elkanah's love for Hannah, not in the least.

At her despair, he asked her, "Hannah, why weep you? And why eat you not? And why is your heart grieved? Am not I better to you than ten sons?" (I Samuel 1:8)

We cannot see the big picture, but God can. He has been through our lives completely, and nothing is a surprise to Him. We only see what is and remember what was, but God is Alpha and Omega, beginning and end. It is difficult, but trust in His timing; it is perfect. "For the revelation awaits an appointed time; it speaks of the end and will not prove false. Though it lingers, wait for it; it will certainly come and will not delay." (Habakkuk 2:3)

I began reading and studying the Bible and writing poetry when I was saved in June of 1998. Words flooded my heart the more time I spent with God and reading His Word. Then in 2000 when I lost my youngest son to a car accident, ironically enough, the Lord gave me my first book to write, and it was called *God's Love*. Boy, did I need it then! He took part of my heart home to be with Him but has given His heart back to me with every word He pours into my heart. I have been writing ever since and wrote one right after the other. I kept wondering, "When Lord, when?" I tried to have the books published once and felt as if I had big red flashing lights going off in my spirit saying, "No!" I knew God was telling me to wait, so I kept writing and kept reading His Word. I wondered from time to time if it would happen and why it was so long in coming. But I also knew the promise I felt in my spirit that He was going to have my books published. After all, the words He gave me seemed to be downloaded into my spirit; I knew they were from Him. So, if He were giving them to me, then He would fulfill His purpose for me in the words He gave me. "The Lord is trustworthy in all He promises and faithful in all he does." (Psalm 145:13) As the years passed, along with more dark trials, I would learn why this goal was so long in coming. With each trial that I came through, God opened my eyes to the things He was teaching me, delivering and healing me from, and more passions He wanted to birth in me. Trust in the process; God was faithful to His promises to me. He did have my books published as He promised, and He brought a publisher to me.

Growth takes time, and nowadays, especially in the United States where we have so many conveniences, we have been a little spoiled. Sometimes we transfer that on to God and want microwaved answers to our prayers. They do not always work that way. Unfortunately, sometimes the answers to our prayers take time, maybe years. We do not like to wait, especially if in the wait, it hurts. But that is where we grow – we grow and learn in perseverance. Year after year Hannah prayed, and year after year, still no children. You might have thought she would have given up, but she persevered all the more.

In the trials of life is where we learn what we are made of, and where our weaknesses lie. God allows only the trials that will help us to grow and grow closer to Him. He will also provide whatever tools and people to encourage us along the way. I remember someone else who endured pain beyond measure, ridicule, beatings, and being spat on, all because people did not believe Him and who He said He was: Jesus Christ.

"See, my servant, will act wisely; He will be raised and lifted up and highly exalted. Just as there were many who were appalled at Him—His appearance was so disfigured beyond that of any human being and His form marred beyond human likeness—so He will sprinkle many nations, and kings will shut their mouths because of Him. For what they were not told, they will see, and what they have not heard, they will understand." (Isaiah 52:13-15)

You and I may never have to endure such pain, but we will have to endure trials that to us, are just as hard. He did it for a very good reason and that is love.

"Greater love has no man than this, that a man lay down his life for his friends."(John 15:13)

So if He had so much overwhelming, unconditional love for us to endure such pain, then know the extreme trial you may be in now, have gone through, or may still yet go through will be for a good reason. Trust Him all through the trial and He will lead you through to victory.

"It was not by their sword that they won the land, nor did their arm bring them victory; it was your right hand, your arm, and the light of your face, for you loved them. You are my King and my god, who decrees victories for Jacob." (Psalm 44:3-4)

5

∽

Despair Sets In

When you have been going through a very long and rough trial it is very easy to get depressed and allow despair to set in. David experienced that when he was sought by King Saul. Saul had disobeyed the Lord and the Lord had departed from him. Saul became jealous of David when he saw how all the people gave him honor. So, he sought to kill him. David spent years running from Saul. Away from home, away from his family, you can imagine how he must have become downhearted at times. "Why, my soul, are you downcast? Why so disturbed within me? Put your hope in God, for I will yet praise Him, my Savior and my God." (Psalm 43:5) But you will find all through the book of Psalms when he was downcast, he always commanded himself to still praise God. God truly becomes your God when He is God of your bad times as well as the good. "The man of God came up and told the king of Israel, 'This is what the Lord says: 'Because the Arameans think the Lord is a god of the hills and not a god of the valleys, I will deliver this vast army into your hands, and you will know that I am the Lord.''" (I Kings 20:28)

Despair can take over, grab hold of your heart, and set in deep. It can last longer than you want it to and if you let it, can be a lot harder to let go of. The only way out is God Almighty! It is taking our eyes off the problem and deciding no matter what, His love on the cross was enough to trust Him through the bad, and even in this difficult and possibly long situation, trust Him anyway. "Trust in the Lord with all your heart and lean not on your own understanding; in all your ways submit to Him, and He will make your paths straight." (Proverbs 3:5-6) To get your eyes off the problem you have to sometimes, make yourself read the Word of God. It is your weapon! "May the praise of God be in their mouths and a double-edged sword in their hands, to inflict vengeance on the nations and punishment on the peoples, to bind their kings with fetters, their nobles with shackles of iron, to carry out the sentence written against them—this is the glory of all His faithful people." (Psalm 149:6-9)

Your mouth is the other weapon. Praise Him! He enters into your presence when you praise! "But you are holy, O you that inhabit the praises of Israel." (Psalm 22:3) That pain, heartache, and despair are darkness, and darkness and the light of Jesus within your heart cannot reside together. "If I say, 'Surely the darkness will hide me, and the light become night around me,' even the darkness will not be dark to You; the night will shine like the day, for darkness is as light to You." (Psalm 139:11-12) And in His presence is joy! "Many, Lord, are asking, 'Who will bring us prosperity?' Let the light of your face shine on us. Fill my heart with joy when their grain and new wine abound." (Psalm 4:6-7)

Job was no stranger to depression and pain, and he went through it for a long time. We do not know exactly how long, but we do not from the Word it was months. "So, I have been allotted months of futility, and nights of misery have been assigned to me." (Job 7:3) Job began the long trial trusting God, but as the months went on, after losing his children and the enduring pain of his illness, despair set in and he began to question God. Even in Job's wrong judgments about God, God showed him mercy and delivered him. "Because of the Lord's loving devotion, we are not consumed, for His compassions never fail. They are new every morning; great is Your faithfulness." (Lamentations 3:22-23) Job was humbled when God spoke to him: "Then Job replied to the Lord: 'I know that You can do all things; no purpose of Yours can be thwarted. You asked, 'Who is this that obscures My plans without knowledge?' Surely, I spoke of things I did not understand, things too wonderful for me to know.

You said, 'Listen now, and I will speak; I will question you, and you shall answer Me.' My ears had heard of You but now my eyes have seen You. Therefore, I despise myself and repent in dust and ashes.'" (Job 42:1-6)

Job repented for his complaints without knowledge and forgave his friends, and the Lord healed him and delivered him. He blessed Job more than before: "The Lord blessed the latter part of Job's life more than the former part." (Job 42:12) We are only finite; God is infinite. We only see the now; God sees all. He has been in our past and our future, and He tells us the end from the beginning. "I make known the end from the beginning, from ancient times, what is still to come. I say, 'My purpose will stand, and I will do all that I please.'" (Isaiah 46:10)

He has a much greater purpose for us in that every detail of our life is worked out and planned, and His ways are much higher than ours. "Seek the Lord while He may be found; call on Him while he is near. Let the wicked forsake their ways and the unrighteous their thoughts. Let them turn to the Lord, and He will have mercy on them, and to our God, for He will freely pardon. 'For my thoughts are not your thoughts, neither are your ways My ways,' declares the Lord. "As the heavens are higher than the earth, so are My ways higher than your ways and My thoughts than your thoughts. As the rain and the snow come down from heaven, and do not return to it without watering the earth and making it bud and flourish, so that it yields seed for the sower and bread for the eater, so is my word that goes out from My mouth: It will not return to Me empty but will accomplish what I desire and achieve the purpose for which I sent it. You will go out in joy and be led forth in peace; the mountains and hills will burst into song before you, and all the trees of the field will clap their hands. Instead of the thornbush, will grow the juniper, and instead of briers, the myrtle will grow. This will be for the Lord's renown, for an everlasting sign, that will endure forever." (Isaiah 55:6-13)

Even though in long and very difficult and painful trials, we allow despair to set in so greatly that we find it hard to pull ourselves out of it, God will never allow, us, His children, to stay that way! "The Lord upholds all who fall and lifts up all who are bowed down." (Psalm 145:14) The beauty of the love and mercy of God is He understands our humanity and has compassion on us. He may have a much greater purpose for allowing the trials we go through, just as He allowed Hannah's barrenness, but He also has compassion on us and delivers and heals us. "The Lord is close to the brokenhearted and saves those who are crushed in spirit. Many are the afflictions of the righteous, but the Lord delivers him from them all." (Psalm 38:18-19)

Hannah prayed year after year for a child and still had none. Her rival, Elkanah's other wife, was able to bear children and would tease Hannah. "This went on year after year. Whenever Hannah went up to the house of the Lord, her rival provoked her till she wept and would not eat." (I Samuel 1:7) This showed the humility of Hannah's spirit. She did not retaliate; she wept, which showed just how tender-hearted she was, but it also made the despair set in even deeper. At that, she would not even eat. Having children was an important part of being married, based on the Lord's command: "And God blessed them, saying, be fruitful, and multiply, and fill the waters in the seas, and let fowl multiply in the earth." (Genesis 1:22) But the fact that Hannah could not have children did not alter Elkanah's overwhelming love for Hannah. He loved her more than the children she could bear, "Her husband Elkanah would say to her, 'Hannah, why are you weeping? Why don't you eat? Why are you downhearted? Don't I mean more to you than ten sons?'" (I Samuel 1:8)

That is the way it is with our Lord. He does not like our sins, but He loves us and died for us while we sinned against Him. "But God demonstrates His own love for us in this: While we were still sinners, Christ died for us." (Romans 5:8) If there is a greater purpose to allow our life to be a testimony, God will allow it. If it will open your eyes to something, God will allow it, and if it will produce a passion for purpose, God will allow it. We just have to trust Him through it and as Mary declared: "I am the Lord's servant,' Mary answered. 'May your word to me be fulfilled.' Then the angel left her." (Luke 1:38) Can you imagine how Mary, a young girl who had never been with a man, felt? Even though an angel appeared, and this would be of God, she still must have been scared of how Joseph would feel and what others would think, yet she decided to trust God.

We need to do the same. "All you Israelites, trust in the Lord-- He is their help and shield." (Psalm 115:9)

God is love, and He cannot go against His true nature, so painful trials in our lives are for a good reason and will produce glorious fruit if we faint not. To everything, there is a season. (Ecclesiastes 3:1) "There is a time for everything and a season for every activity under the heavens." So, there must have been a purpose for Hannah to go through this painful trial, one that would draw something out of her and one that would bear much fruit, and in the process bring her great joy. There will be fruit harvested from your trial as well! It is promised! (Psalm 1:3) "That person is like a tree planted by streams of water, which yields its fruit in season and whose leaf does not wither-- whatever they do prospers." Just as Paul describes in his letter to the Ephesians, his suffering turned out for God's glory, to benefit others. "I ask you, therefore, not to be discouraged because of my sufferings for you, which are your glory." (Ephesians 3:13)

The depths of Elkanah's love for Hannah and her emotional well-being are shown in how he puts her happiness over having children. This depicts the love of God in that He gave His one and only Son to be the atonement for our sins. "For God so loved the world that He gave His one and only Son, that whoever believes in Him shall not perish but have eternal life. For God did not send His Son into the world to condemn the world, but to save the world through Him. Whoever believes in Him is not condemned, but whoever does not believe stands condemned already because they have not believed in the name of God's one and only Son. This is the verdict: Light has come into the world, but people loved darkness instead of light because their deeds were evil. Everyone who does evil hates the light and will not come into the light for fear that their deeds will be exposed. But whoever lives by the truth comes into the light, so that it may be seen plainly that what they have done has been done in the sight of God." (John 3:16-21)

Jesus gave up the comforts of heaven to come to earth in human form to understand us and to be the atonement for our sins, yet He, Himself was sinless. He was ridiculed, spit on, beaten, and hung on the cross for healing people and sharing the good news. He gave up His comfort for us: "Therefore if you have any encouragement from being united with Christ, if any comfort from His love, if any common sharing in the Spirit, if any tenderness and compassion, then make my joy complete by being like-minded, having the same love, being one in spirit and of one mind. Do nothing out of selfish ambition or vain conceit. Rather, in humility value others above yourselves, not looking to your own interests but each of you to the interests of the others. In your relationships with one another, have the same mindset as Christ Jesus: Who, being in very nature God, did not consider equality with God something to be used to His own advantage; rather, He made Himself nothing by taking the very nature of a servant, being made in human likeness. And being found in appearance as a man, He humbled Himself by becoming obedient to death—even death on a cross! Therefore, God exalted Him to the highest place and gave Him the name that is above every name, that at the name of Jesus, every knee should bow, in heaven and on earth and under the earth, and every tongue acknowledge that Jesus Christ is Lord, to the glory of God the Father." (Philippians 2:1-11)

Because of His unselfish act of love, through the fruit of His Holy Spirit within us, we can call on His strength to lift us up in our time of need. "But the fruit of the Spirit is love, joy, peace, forbearance, kindness, goodness, faithfulness, gentleness and self-control. Against such things, there is no law. Those who belong to Christ Jesus have crucified the flesh with its passions and desires. Since we live by the Spirit, let us keep in step with the Spirit." (Galatians 5:22-25)

It does not matter if the trial is to open your eyes to something you are doing or not doing, to sin, or to birth a passion for purpose in you out of this trial, you have what you need with the Holy Spirit within you, and you can make it through this trial. His joy is your strength! "Nehemiah said, 'Go and enjoy choice food and sweet drinks, and send some to those who have nothing prepared. This day is holy to our Lord. Do not grieve, for the joy of the Lord is your strength.'" (Nehemiah 8:10)

The pain from the trial you are going through may have effects on your attitude, faith, and endurance that you may not even be aware of and may affect those who see you day in and day out. Paul used to have

Christians killed, but he was saved and wrote thirteen books in the New Testament, and half of those were from prison! He made a difference. People in prison were saved!

"About midnight Paul and Silas were praying and singing hymns to God, and the other prisoners were listening to them. Suddenly there was such a violent earthquake that the foundations of the prison were shaken. At once all the prison doors flew open, and everyone's chains came loose. The jailer woke up, and when he saw the prison doors open, he drew his sword and was about to kill himself because he thought the prisoners had escaped. But Paul shouted, 'Don't harm yourself! We are all here!' The jailer called for lights, rushed in, and fell trembling before Paul and Silas. He then brought them out and asked, 'Sirs, what must I do to be saved?' They replied, 'Believe in the Lord Jesus, and you will be saved—you and your household.' (Acts 16:25-31)

Paul wrote the book of Philippians during his Roman imprisonment in AD 61 and Roman citizens of Caesar's household were saved: "All God's people here send you greetings, especially those who belong to Caesar's household." (Philippians 4:22)

Ask the Lord for help and wisdom as you go through difficult trials. He will give generously. Your attitude through it may be more of a witness than you think.

"You then, my son, be strong in the grace that is in Christ Jesus. And the things you have heard me say in the presence of many witnesses entrust to reliable people who will also be qualified to teach others. Join with me in suffering, like a good soldier of Christ Jesus. No one serving as a soldier gets entangled in civilian affairs, but rather tries to please his commanding officer. Similarly, anyone who competes as an athlete does not receive the victor's crown except by competing according to the rules. The hardworking farmer should be the first to receive a share of the crops. Reflect on what I am saying, for the Lord will give you insight into all this. Remember Jesus

Christ, raised from the dead, descended from David. This is my gospel, for which I am suffering even to the point of being chained like a criminal. But God's word is not chained. Therefore, I endure everything for the sake of the elect, that they too may obtain the salvation that is in Christ Jesus, with eternal glory. Here is a trustworthy saying: If we died with Him, we will also live with Him; if we endure, we will also reign with Him. If we disown Him, He will also disown us; if we are faithless, He remains faithful, for He cannot disown Himself." (II Timothy 2:1-13)

6

Why?

After the despair comes the confusion, and the "whys." The "Why is this taking so long" and "Why me Lord, what did I do?" I am sure the same question went through Hannah's mind as well. She had gone through years of barrenness, years of praying for a child, years of enduring the provoking of Peninnah, and still no child.

Had Hannah done something wrong? I'm sure this question added to the despair and the "whys." Looking into what the first chapter of Samuel gives us, Hannah's character does not fit being disciplined, and the meaning of her name further agrees. Hannah is from the Hebrew *Channah,* meaning "favor." When Peninnah provoked her, she wept, which showed that her heart was not mean-spirited, vengeful, or arrogant, deserving discipline. She was tender-hearted. Yet, the Lord closed her womb. So, it must have been for another reason other than discipline. What was it? To discover the answer to this question, a deeper look is needed. Why do we go through trials? Many different reasons; one being the consequences of our own free will and bad choices, or someone else's. Another is that God may want to draw something out of us and give us a revelation that we can only receive going through this specific trial. And there are seasons of them – there is a beginning and an end, and God always promises that we are overcomers! "You, dear children, are from

God and have overcome them because the one who is in you is greater than the one who is in the world." (I John 4:4)

The meaning of Hannah's name, favor, means this had to be for a purpose that would bear fruit. Oh, the love of God that He should choose any of us to bear fruit for His almighty purpose! "You did not choose Me, but I chose you and appointed you so that you might go and bear fruit--fruit that will last--and so that whatever you ask in My name the Father will give you." (John 15:16)

The fruit she would bear would bring much glory to God, and we were all created for His glory. "I will say to the north, 'Give them up!' and to the south, 'Do not hold them back!' Bring My sons from afar, and My daughters from the ends of the earth—everyone who is called by my name, whom I created for my glory, whom I formed and made." (Isaiah 43:6-7) We all have a purpose, and each of us will bring much glory when we are fulfilling our purpose through Jesus Christ. "For we are God's handiwork, created in Christ Jesus to do good works, which God prepared in advance for us to do." (Ephesians 2:10)

It may be that God has called you to be a witness in your home, extended family members, and the job arena. Your pastor cannot be everywhere, and you may not realize just how important that is – we see more people in our everyday lives than a Pastor will see on a Sunday. It may be He has called you to sing His praises professionally or to be a preacher or evangelist. Whatever it is, every single calling of God is important, they all fit together, and He makes the seeds planted grow. (I Corinthians 3:7) "So neither the one who plants nor the one who waters is anything, but only God, who makes things grow." The earth will pass away but where we spend eternity and who we take with us matters. Eternity, our next life, is forever and as we love our children – we were made in the image of God – He loves all He has made and wants us all with Him. "This is good and pleasing in the sight of God our Savior, who wants all people to be saved and to come to a knowledge of the truth." (I Timothy 2:3-4)

But there had to be more. God had a purpose. What was it? "But to Hannah he gave a double portion because he loved her, and the Lord had closed her womb." (I Samuel 1:5) The Hebrew meaning of the word "closed" (shut up) means, **"surrender, deliver, give over, pure, enclose, repair, confined, isolate."** Wow! So many different meanings. Let's go even deeper. Let's look at **surrender and deliver.** What happens when you surrender your life to Christ? You are saved and born again! What next? Your lifestyle changes; you have a strong desire to know more about God. You go to church, you read the Bible, you pray, and talk to Him. You draw close to Him. What happened to Hannah? What did she do when she was overcome with despair at not being able to have children? She drew closer to God; she sought Him more deeply. What else happens as we draw closer to God? Our eyes are opened to our past ways and the ways of our "worldly" friends, or those who are not as committed, those friends who may not be saved. The things we once did, like maybe clubbing, do not interest us any longer. We separate ourselves or **isolate ourselves**.

"Therefore, 'Come out from them and be separate, says the Lord. Touch no unclean thing, and I will receive you.'" (II Corinthians 6:17) Sound familiar? One of the meanings of "closed/shut up" is to **isolate and enclose.** You isolate yourself from the temptations or bad influences you were once around daily. You have no desire for them any longer. Your desire now is to please God and to draw closer to Him. As you do, you begin to grow spiritually. The trials that you go through in the maturing process remove your character defects, which will harm or stunt your spiritual growth. "In this, you greatly rejoice, though now for a little while you may have had to suffer various trials. These have come so that the proven genuineness of your faith--of greater worth than gold, which perishes even though refined by fire--may result in praise, glory, and honor when Jesus Christ is revealed." (I Peter 1:6-7) This is purifying your heart and soul, which is also one of the meanings: **"pure."**

"Consider it pure joy, my brothers, and sisters, whenever you face trials of many kinds because you know that the testing of your faith produces perseverance. Let perseverance finish its work so that you may be mature and complete, not lacking anything. If any of you lacks wisdom, you should ask God, who gives generously to all without finding fault, and it will be given to you." (James 1:2-5)

Hannah's perseverance through her trial should give us the courage to continue in ours. God saw her heart, and so did Elkanah. The way Elkanah loved Hannah even though she could not bear him any children is just like God's love for us in that even before we reach our spiritual maturity or our purpose in Him, in His overwhelming love for us He still gives us a double portion! The double portion is first the indwelling at conversion. "Because you are his sons, God sent the Spirit of his Son into our hearts, the Spirit who calls out, 'Abba, Father.'" (Galatians 4:6) The other portion is the baptism of the Holy Spirit. As we **"surrender,"** which is another one of our word definitions, and seek Him with our whole heart, and ask, our Lord baptizes us with His Holy Spirit. "But you will receive power when the Holy Spirit comes on you, and you will be my witnesses in Jerusalem, and in all Judea and Samaria, and to the ends of the earth." (Acts 1:8) When you are baptized in the Holy Spirit, His Spirit comes on you and totally consumes you! How great is our God! Hannah had been called by God to give birth to His purpose, which would help many and anoint kings. Just like Mary gave birth to Jesus, who died to save our souls through His death, upon us believing and receiving, the Holy Spirit is deposited in us and His fruit is birthed in us! "Whoever believes in Me, as Scripture has said, rivers of living water will flow from within them." (John 7:38) Through all her barrenness, this was a privilege that God would use her. "Yet if any man suffers as a Christian, let him not be ashamed; but let him glorify God on this behalf." (I Peter 4:16)

Trials are painful, and some bring heartache, but if they are allowed by God, the one who died in our place, then it is for a good reason. "For our light and momentary troubles are achieving for us an eternal glory that far outweighs them all." (II Corinthians 4:17) I went through years of feeling as if I did not matter, or was invisible and did not deserve to be happy due to the situation I was in, but through it, the Lord found me and as the situation continued it caused me to draw closer and closer to God. I needed His strength and the wisdom of the Lord through the Bible. "But those who wait upon the Lord will renew their strength; they will mount up with wings like eagles; they will run and not grow weary; they will walk and not faint." (Isaiah 40:31)

The Word of God is living and active, and it gave me strength to endure. A hunger and passion to read and study the Bible was birthed in me. The strength of God I found through the Bible not only helped me to persevere, it gave me wisdom to know how to handle the hand life through at me. "If any of you lacks wisdom, you should ask God, who gives generously to all without finding fault, and it will be given to you." (James 1:5) I needed that strength again, to get past the loss of my son. God carried me and my heart in His hands until I was strong enough to want to go on again. Through it all, God would not let me give up. He would have a friend of mine continually give me encouragement along with the love of my family.

In Hannah's despair, I am sure God encouraged her heart as well. "For this is what the Lord says: 'I will extend peace to her like a river, and the wealth of nations like a flowing stream; you will nurse and be carried on her arm and bounced upon her knees. As a mother comforts her child, so will I comfort you; and you will be comforted over Jerusalem.' When you see this, your heart will rejoice, and you will flourish like grass; the hand of the Lord will be made known to His servants, but His fury will be shown to His foes." (Isaiah 66:12-14) As a child of God, even if the trial is for discipline as well as purpose, God will be our strength and soothe our broken hearts until the victory is ours.

When children of God suffer through trials and hardships and stay committed to Him, He promises that they will reap a harvest. "Let us not become weary in doing good, for at the proper time we will reap a harvest if we do not give up." (Galatians 6:9) I persevered, I never gave up believing that God would come through for me. Through all the years of hardship and the loss of my son, I continued to stay close to God, and I continued to read the Bible. All along, God was birthing something in me, although I was unaware. He was equipping me with what I needed for the gift He would manifest through me, writing. "Now may the God of peace, who through the blood of the eternal covenant brought back from the dead our Lord Jesus, the great Shepherd of the sheep, equip you with everything good for doing his will, and may he work in us what is pleasing to him, through Jesus Christ, to whom be glory forever and ever. Amen." (Hebrews 13:20-21) At the time I was saved, He poured words into me and I began writing poetry. I never had a desire to write books until my son died. That was when He gave me my first book, and at the time of this book I have written 22 books, and I am working on more. I never had a clue.

I am sure that Hannah did not understand what purpose God would have for the son she was praying for, either, yet she prayed and prayed. Hannah drew closer to God in prayer and just possibly, that is what God wanted. Would she have pressed in so intently if having children were not a problem? Hannah went to the temple and poured her heart out to God, never receiving an answer for her "whys." "Once when they had finished eating and drinking in Shiloh, Hannah stood up. Now Eli the priest was sitting on his chair by the doorpost of the Lord's house. In her deep anguish, Hannah prayed to the Lord, weeping bitterly." (I Samuel 1:9-10) Hannah wept before the Lord and she prayed year after year. She never gave up! "Then Jesus told His disciples a parable to show them that they should always pray and not give up." (Luke 18:1)

Don't give up on God if you are going through a difficult trial. Victory is promised, and God is faithful. He will deliver you as He did me, as He did Job, and as He did Hannah and many, many more in the Bible.

"Not one of all the Lord's good promises to Israel failed; every one was fulfilled. (Joshua 21:45)

7

Pressing In

Hannah's barrenness continued year after year, and yet she did not give up; she got stubborn! Sounds a lot like myself; I refuse to give up, I refuse to allow the enemy to win. He has caused enough trouble in my life and I am not going to give him the satisfaction of stealing my purpose! What he meant for bad, God is going to take the mess, the destruction, the loss and restore it to make something beautiful out of it! What better way to get back at the enemy and allow your trials to turn into a testimony to reach many people! "And we know that all things work together for good to them that love God, to them who are the called according to His purpose." (Romans 8:28)

A beautiful example of this is a favorite pastime of mine: making candles. They give off a beautiful glow and a sense of peace. They can be easily purchased, but in making them, you get to add your own touch to them. To start you need wax, something to melt it in, the coloring you want, and your scent. You also need a candle mold, wick, and mold release. The mold release helps the candle to come out of the mold with ease once it is set. The Holy Spirit is ours, He helps us to go through our trials with ease when we rely on Him. "But he said to me, 'My grace is sufficient for you, for My power is made perfect in weakness.' Therefore, I will boast all the more gladly about my weaknesses, so that Christ's power may rest on me." (II Corinthians 12:9) The wax as it melts is us in our trials under the heat of affliction. "Praise be to the God and Father of our Lord Jesus Christ! In His great mercy, He has given us new birth into a living hope through the resurrection of Jesus Christ from the dead, and into an inheritance that can never perish, spoil or fade. This inheritance is kept in heaven for you, who through faith are shielded by God's power until the coming of the salvation that is ready to be revealed in the last time. In all this, you greatly rejoice, though now for a little while you may have had to suffer grief in all kinds of trials. These have come so that the proven genuineness of your faith—of greater worth than gold, which perishes even though refined by fire—may result in praise, glory, and honor when Jesus Christ is revealed. Though you have not seen Him, you love Him; and even though you do not see Him now, you believe in Him and are filled with an inexpressible and glorious joy, for you are receiving the end result of your faith, the salvation of your souls." (I Peter 1:3-8)

As the wax melts you add the coloring and the scent that you want. The trials we go through will add color to us. We learn and grow into spiritual maturity, and purpose is birthed in us through trials. "For you, God, tested us; you refined us like silver." (Psalm 66:10)

Once the wax is melted, you spray the mold release into the mold, pour in the melted wax, and set the wick in place. There are many different things you can do to add your special touch. You can leave the wax clear without color and break up other old used candles of different colors into pieces to add to the mold before pouring in the melted wax. When set, you can see the colored pieces through the clear wax candle. It lights beautifully! Another thing you can do is add ice cubes to the mold before pouring the melted wax. When it melts, there is a hole left in the candle wherever the ice melts. The candle looks like Swiss cheese, but it gives off even more of a glow when lit! Sounds like us after we have come through a trial victoriously. All those cracks that were in our hearts, leave more room for God to shine through us! "Out of Zion, the perfection of beauty, God has shined." (Psalm 50:2)

In Hannah's barrenness, she sought the Lord more intensely and passionately. Her barrenness caused her to press in, to seek God and the answer to her prayer with more passion. "As she kept on praying to the Lord, Eli observed her mouth. Hannah was praying in her heart, and her lips were moving but her voice was not heard. Eli thought she was drunk and said to her, 'How long are you going to stay drunk? Put away your wine.' 'Not so, my lord,' Hannah replied, 'I am a woman who is deeply troubled. I have not been drinking wine or beer; I was pouring out my soul to the Lord. Do not take your servant for a wicked woman; I have been praying here out of my great anguish and grief.' (I Samuel 1:12-16) This might not have happened otherwise, if the Lord had not closed her womb. God knows the end from the beginning. "I make known the end from the beginning, from ancient times, what is still to come. I say, 'My purpose will stand, and I will do all that I please.'" (Isaiah 46:10) God knew what it would take, He knew the determination of Hannah in pursuing the answer to her prayer to have a child and when to bless her with the answer. "I am the Alpha and the Omega, the First and the Last, the Beginning and the End." (Revelation 22:13)

He knows exactly what is needed and when to heal, save, deliver, and perfect our hearts and what will draw the passion out of us for His purpose and glory. "He said, 'Can I not do with you, Israel, as this potter does?' declares the Lord. 'Like clay in the hand of the potter, so are you in my hand, Israel.'" (Jeremiah 18:6) He has been through our trials ahead of us. "But be assured today that the Lord your God is the one who goes across ahead of you like a devouring fire. He will destroy them; he will subdue them before you. And you will drive them out and annihilate them quickly, as the Lord has promised you." (Deuteronomy 9:3)

God knows our hearts and who will passionately pursue Him and serve Him wholeheartedly. The trial you are going through may be what God is using to draw something out of you, just like Hannah. She did not do anything wrong. If your heart does not condemn you, then it may be God is trying to teach you something or draw a passion out of you for His purpose. "If our hearts condemn us, we know that God is greater than our hearts, and he knows everything." (I John 3:20)

Hannah did not become angry, resentful, or bitter at being barren. Instead, she pursued God even harder. What a beautiful story God has given us in this one verse: "And the Lord closed her womb." If you seek Him, if you ask for wisdom and go deeper, He will give it to you! I would have missed this beautiful story if I had passed this verse by as I read. When the Holy Spirit tugs at you as you read the Word, stop at that passage and stay awhile. You do not know what treasures you may be missing by reading through and not stopping to dig deeper. This is not only about the great love God and Elkanah had for Hannah, but His great love for us as well. God knew her heart and knew she had the endurance to see it through and pursue Him on a deeper level.

Nehemiah and Ezra faced a lot of opposition when they set out to restore the temple, walls, and gates of Jerusalem. After the exile of the Israelites, Nehemiah was troubled by the state of disrepair of the walls and gates of Jerusalem. This is a symbol of our own broken hearts and relationship with God. God wants to restore and repair. "Your people will rebuild the ancient ruins and will raise up the age-old foundations; you will be called Repairer of Broken Walls, Restorer of Streets with Dwellings." (Isaiah 58:12) God impressed upon Nehemiah's heart to repair the wall. He faced a lot of opposition and those sent by the enemy to stop it. Nehemiah did not fall for any of their tactics and pressed on and it was finally completed. Ezra oversaw the rebuilding of the Temple. God had laid it on the heart of the King of Persia, of all people, who was not even of Jewish descent! God can use anyone, any time, to fulfill His purpose! "In the first year of Cyrus king of Persia, in order to fulfill the word of the Lord spoken by Jeremiah, the Lord moved the heart of Cyrus king of Persia to make a proclamation throughout his realm and also to put it in writing: 'This is what Cyrus king of Persia says: 'The Lord, the God of heaven, has given me all the kingdoms of the earth and He has appointed me to build a temple for Him at Jerusalem in Judah. Any of His people among you may go up to Jerusalem in Judah and build the temple of the Lord, the God of Israel, the God who is in Jerusalem, and may their God be with them. And in any locality where survivors may now be living, the people are to provide them with silver and gold, with goods and livestock, and with freewill offerings for the temple of God in Jerusalem.'" (Ezra 1:1-4)

Ezra faced a lot of opposition as well, and it was stopped, but only temporarily. If God commands it, if it is His purpose, He will make sure it gets done. "I make known the end from the beginning, from ancient times, what is still to come. I say, 'My purpose will stand, and I will do all that I please.'" (Isaiah 46:10) The temple was completed. If He has a purpose for you, your life, and the trial you may be facing, call out to Him for help, He will surely provide. "Pray you therefore the Lord of the harvest, that He will send forth laborers into His harvest." (Matthew 9:38)

In I Samuel 1, we see that Hannah had this same determination. It seemed that as the years passed, she did not want to quit, but she pressed in even harder. She set it in her mind and heart to see it through and not give up. "I will bless the Lord, who has given me counsel: my heart also instructs me in the night seasons. I have set the Lord always before me: because He is at my right hand, I shall not be moved. Therefore, my heart is glad, and my glory rejoices: my flesh also shall rest in hope." (Psalm 16:7-9) If we are to pass through our trials victoriously and not set up a camp of self-pity, then we are going to have to develop this same attitude and think to ourselves. "I will not be shaken, I will not be moved!"

David was another person from the Bible who had a long and difficult trial. King Saul pursued him for years out of jealousy to kill him. The Lord provided people in his path to help him as well as his needs. David did nothing wrong; he served the Lord and lived with integrity, and the Lord showed him favor when King Saul disobeyed him. The Lord purposed to set David as the next king and even said of David, even though he was not perfect by any means, he was "A man after My own heart." (Acts 13:22) The Psalms recorded David's emotions as he ran from Saul. He did not give up and even had a chance to kill Saul himself, but chose not to: "He said to his men, 'The Lord forbid that I should do such a thing to my master, the Lord's anointed, or lay my hand on him; for he is the anointed of the Lord.'" (I Samuel 24:6) God rewarded David's perseverance and integrity, and he was made king.

In answer to the question of Hannah's barrenness, it was not to discipline her or punish her. It was the love and devotion of God to bless her! Your trial will bring blessings as well. God saw her heart and humility and through her barrenness, she sought the Lord more intensely in order to bear a son. In her prayer to have a son, she made a promise to God. This was a promise she would keep, and her joy would be complete!

"Those who sow with tears will reap with songs of joy." (Psalm 126:5)

8

～

The Promise

Hannah pressed in as time passed, and still did not give up on her desire and prayer to have a child. She was so determined that now, she made a promise to God. If Hannah had not been barren, this might not have happened. She would not have been so desperate to seek the Lord at a deeper level and promise her firstborn son to God. "Once when they had finished eating and drinking in Shiloh, Hannah stood up. Now Eli the priest was sitting on his chair by the doorpost of the Lord's house. In her deep anguish, Hannah prayed to the Lord, weeping bitterly. And she made a vow, saying, 'Lord Almighty, if You will only look on Your servant's misery and remember me, and not forget your servant but give her a son, then I will give him to the Lord for all the days of his life, and no razor will ever be used on his head.'" (I Samuel 1:9-11)

Are you going through a difficult trial? Call on the Lord, go to Him in prayer, and ask for wisdom and strength. He will help you through it. "But those who hope in the Lord will renew their strength. They will soar on wings like eagles; they will run and not grow weary, they will walk and not be faint." (Isaiah 40:31) The more passionate you are about the purpose and desire of your heart, the more determined you will be also to not give up, to keep pursuing regardless of the cost. The more you pursue, the clearer and clearer the purpose becomes as well. Problems will

58

arise, and time will go by, just like it did for Nehemiah and Ezra. They saw the rebuilding of the Temple and the wall of Jerusalem through, even with all the opposition, and the rebuilding was finally completed.

Even though sometimes the trials may last a long time, you will learn something if you surrender your heart and your will to God. If you humble yourself and ask Him to open your eyes to what He wants to teach you through them, He will teach you and give you fresh revelations. "His divine power has given us everything we need for a godly life through our knowledge of Him who called us by His own glory and goodness. Through these He has given us His very great and precious promises, so that through them you may participate in the divine nature, having escaped the corruption in the world caused by evil desires. For this very reason, make every effort to add to your faith goodness; and to goodness, knowledge; and to knowledge, self-control; and to self-control, perseverance; and to perseverance, godliness; and to godliness, mutual affection; and to mutual affection, love. For if you possess these qualities in increasing measure, they will keep you from being ineffective and unproductive in your knowledge of our Lord Jesus Christ. But whoever does not have them is nearsighted and blind, forgetting that they have been cleansed from their past sins. Therefore, my brothers and sisters, make every effort to confirm your calling and election. For if you do these things, you will never stumble, and you will receive a rich welcome into the eternal kingdom of our Lord and Savior Jesus Christ." (II Peter 1:3-11)

You will finally learn to surrender and submit to His will, and in doing this you grow more and more to spiritual maturity. When you learn to seek Him and His will over yours it will draw you closer and closer to the manifestation of the promise, the answer to your prayers. "But seek first His kingdom and His righteousness, and all these things will be given to you as well." (Matthew 6:33)

Through all the turmoil in my life, the darkness, the people that made me feel worthless, and such darkness that I even despaired life itself, God would not let me give up. God showed me over and over through both of my sons or a friend that He loved me and "He would not fail or forsake me." When you are too weak and too tired to carry on, He will be your strength. "I have found David My servant; with My sacred oil, I have anointed him. My hand will sustain him; surely My arm will strengthen him. The enemy will not get the better of him; the wicked will not oppress him. I will crush his foes before him and strike down his adversaries. My faithful love will be with him, and through My name, his horn will be exalted." (Psalm 89:20-24) God would not allow me to give up when my own strength failed. Time and time again God picked me up and held my heart in His hands.

Hannah was so determined she promised her firstborn to the Lord, that she made a vow. "In her deep anguish, Hannah prayed to the Lord, weeping bitterly. And she made a vow, saying, 'Lord Almighty, if you will only look on your servant's misery and remember me, and not forget your servant but give her a son, then I will give him to the Lord for all the days of his life, and no razor will ever be used on his head.'" (I Samuel 1:10-11) This was pure determination; the Jewish people were taught by the Lord to not make a vow you could not keep. So, for her to make a vow was huge; it showed how important having her prayer answered was to her. "If you make a vow to the Lord your God, do not be slow to pay it, for the Lord your God will certainly demand it of you and you will be guilty of sin." (Deuteronomy 23:21)

Ruth was someone else in the Bible who was determined. Ruth lived in Moab and was married to Naomi's son Mahlon. Naomi, her husband Elimelek, and her two sons had moved to Moab from Bethlehem, Judah. There was a famine in the land, and instead of going to the Lord in prayer, Naomi and Elimelek just moved; they moved to Moab. That is a story in itself. Bethlehem means "place of bread," and they moved away from it, their place of bread in a time of drought. There are times when God is silent, but He is still there. He may be using this time to draw you closer to Him. Naomi and Elimelek moved to Moab, and their two sons married women from Moab. Then, all three men died: Elimelek, Mahlon, and their other son, Kilion. This left Naomi alone, or so she thought. But even though her family moved from Bethlehem, Naomi did not stop following God. It showed and made a difference. Ruth took notice, and when Naomi decided to return to Bethlehem, Ruth was determined to go with her. Watch what you say and how you act in your trial; you do not know who is watching and listening, and what a difference it will make. Naomi's faith, even through all of this and even when she became discouraged at losing everyone she loved, still made a difference; it had a lasting effect.

"Then Naomi said to her two daughters-in-law, 'Go back, each of you, to your mother's home. May the Lord show you kindness, as you have shown kindness to your dead husbands and to me. May the Lord grant that each of you will find rest in the home of another husband.' Then she kissed them goodbye and they wept aloud and said to her, 'We will go back with you to your people.' But Naomi said, 'Return home, my daughters. Why would you come with me? Am I going to have any more sons, who could become your husbands? Return home, my daughters; I am too old to have another husband. Even if I thought there was still hope for me—even if I had a husband tonight and then gave birth to sons —would you wait until they grew up? Would you remain unmarried for them? No, my daughters. It is more bitter for me than for you, because the Lord's hand has turned against me!' At this, they wept aloud again. Then Orpah kissed her mother-in-law goodbye, but Ruth clung to her. 'Look,' said Naomi, 'your sister-in-law is going back to her people and her gods. Go back with her.' But Ruth replied, 'Don't urge me to leave you or to turn back from you. Where you go I will go, and where you stay I will stay. Your people will be my people and your God my God. Where you die I will die, and there I will be buried. May the Lord deal with me, be it ever so severely, if even death separates you and me.' When Naomi realized that Ruth was determined to go with her, she stopped urging her." (Ruth 1:8-18)

Naomi stopped urging Ruth to go back home and the two set off back to Bethlehem. Ruth began gleaning in the fields of none other than Boaz, who was the family's kinsman-redeemer. A kinsman-redeemer is one who is next in line to redeem their relative. It is their obligation to take care of them in serious difficulty. Jesus Christ is our Redeemer. Boaz knew who Ruth was, and her faithfulness to her mother-in-law made an impression on him. They ended up getting married, had a child, and named him

Obed, who was in the lineage of David, who was in the lineage of Jesus Christ. "So, Boaz took Ruth and she became his wife. When he made love to her, the Lord enabled her to conceive, and she gave birth to a son. The women said to Naomi: 'Praise be to the Lord, who this day has not left you without a kinsman-redeemer. May he become famous through-out Israel! He will renew your life and sustain you in your old age. For your daughter-in-law, who loves you and who is better to you than seven sons, has given him birth.' Then Naomi took the child in her arms and cared for him. The women living there said, 'Naomi has a son!' And they named him Obed. He was the father of Jesse, the father of David. This, then, is the family line of Perez: Perez was the father of Hezron, Hezron the father of Ram, Ram the father of Amminadab, Amminadab the father of Nahshon, Nahshon the father of Salmon, Salmon the father of Boaz, Boaz the father of Obed, Obed the father of Jesse, and Jesse the father of David." (Ruth 4:13-22)

All through the Bible there are stories of God's faithfulness to His promises and the promises and prayers of His people. They had their ups and downs, their times of faithfulness to God, and their times in which they disobeyed and needed discipline. Regardless, God always provided and always welcomed them back with open arms. The book of Hosea is a story that symbolizes God's love for Israel. His love in caring for them, His love in His discipline, and His love in His mercy to restore. He tells Hosea to take a harlot for a wife to represent Israel's unfaithfulness to Him. "When the Lord began to speak through Hosea, the Lord said to him, 'Go, marry a promiscuous woman and have children with her, for like an adulterous wife this land is guilty of unfaithfulness to the Lord.' Hosea obeyed and married Gomer and they had children, but Gomer would not stay faithful to Hosea. Hosea wanted to give up on her, but God would not let him. 'The Lord said to me, 'Go, show your love to your wife again, though she is loved by another man and is an adulteress. Love her as the Lord loves the Israelites, though they turn to other gods and love the sacred raisin cakes.'" (Hosea 3:1) God would not let Hosea give up on Gomer as a way to tell Israel that even though He may dis-cipline them, He will show mercy and restore them to Himself. He will never give up on the promises He made to them, even though, through their back-and-forth obedience, they may take a while to fulfill. He will never give up on us either, and He will help us and inspire us to stay strong even when we want to quit, just as Hosea did.

Your greatest trial may birth your greatest victory! "Therefore, I am now going to allure her; I will lead her into the wilderness and speak tenderly to her. There I will give her back her vineyards and will make the Valley of Achor a door of hope. There she will respond as in the days of her youth, as in the day she came up out of Egypt." (Hosea 2:14-15) Learn to look at your trials in a new light; they may be a blessing in disguise. Achor is from the Hebrew word, *Akor* meaning, "disturbance." That trial that you're going through right now, ask God to open your eyes to what He wants to teach you or desire He wants to birth in you through this; there may be a gem waiting to be birthed within that trial and a banquet He is preparing for you!

"The Lord is my shepherd, I lack nothing. He makes me lie down in green pastures,

He leads me beside quiet waters, He refreshes my soul. He guides me along the right paths for His name's sake. Even though I walk through the darkest valley, I will fear no evil, for You are with me; Your rod and Your staff, they comfort me. You prepare a table before me in the presence of my enemies. You anoint my head with oil; my cup overflows. Surely Your goodness and love will follow me all the days of my life, and I will dwell in the house of the Lord forever." (Psalm 23)

Stay faithful and determined even when the trial gets difficult. A great promise may be waiting to be birthed in and through you because of the trials and tribulations you face. Hannah had a great purpose waiting to be birthed in her and it was as if her spirit within knew it because she never gave up.

This is a beautiful love story that speaks to all of us. The next time you are going through a difficult season, God may be trying to birth something wonderful in you!

9

Birth!

There is a time and a season for everything, even though the trial may be long and difficult. "For there is a proper time and procedure for every matter, though a person may be weighed down by misery." (Ecclesiastes 8:6) Things have to be right, just like giving birth to a baby. The baby needs to stay in its mother's womb until fully formed. Whether we like it or not, the trial is our womb, and God will not allow the birth of our dream until the right moment. There may still be things we need to learn and overcome that will be necessary for our purpose, and things we still need to be delivered from that may hinder us if we do not get rid of them beforehand. Once in our purpose, God wants us to stay there, prosper in it, and not fall. The length of the trial is actually for your protection. "So, if you think you are standing firm, be careful that you don't fall! No temptation has overtaken you except what is common to mankind. And God is faithful; He will not let you be tempted beyond what you can bear. But when you are tempted, He will also provide a way out so that you can endure it." (I Corinthians 10:12-13)

When it is time, He will let you know; you will sense it in your spirit and you will see that things begin to line up physically. "The Lord our God said to us at Horeb, 'You have stayed long enough at this mountain.'"

(Deuteronomy 1:6) Then suddenly He will act, and everything will fall into place. "I foretold the former things long ago, My mouth announced them, and I made them known; then suddenly I acted, and they came to pass." (Isaiah: 48:3)

Hannah finally gave birth to Samuel, and more besides! She stayed faithful through the despair and the why's and God abundantly blessed her. "And the Lord was gracious to Hannah; she gave birth to three sons and two daughters." (I Samuel 2:21)

"As she kept on praying to the Lord, Eli observed her mouth. Hannah was praying in her heart, and her lips were moving but her voice was not heard. Eli thought she was drunk and said to her, 'How long are you going to stay drunk? Put away your wine.' 'Not so, my lord,' Hannah replied, 'I am a woman who is deeply troubled. I have not been drinking wine or beer; I was pouring out my soul to the Lord. Do not take your servant for a wicked woman; I have been praying here out of my great anguish and grief.' Eli answered, 'Go in peace, and may the God of Israel grant you what you have asked of Him.' She said, 'May your servant find favor in your eyes.' Then she went her way and ate something, and her face was no longer downcast. Early the next morning they arose and worshiped before the Lord and then went back to their home at Ramah. Elkanah made love to his wife Hannah, and the Lord remembered her. So, in the course of time, Hannah became pregnant and gave birth to a son. She named him Samuel, saying, 'Because I asked the Lord for him.'

Hannah Dedicates Samuel

When her husband Elkanah went up with all his family to offer the annual sacrifice to the Lord and to fulfill his vow, Hannah did not go. She said to her husband, 'After the boy is weaned, I will take him and present him before the Lord, and he will live there always.' 'Do what seems best to you,' her husband Elkanah told her. 'Stay here until you have weaned him; only may the Lord make good His word.' So, the woman stayed at home and nursed her son until she had weaned him. After he was weaned, she took the boy with her, young as he was, along with a three-year-old bull, an ephah of flour, and a skin of wine, and brought him to the house of the

Lord at Shiloh. When the bull had been sacrificed, they brought the boy to Eli, and she said to him, 'Pardon me, my lord. As surely as you live, I am the woman who stood here beside you praying to the Lord. I prayed for this child, and the Lord has granted me what I asked of Him. So now I give him to the Lord. For his whole life, he will be given over to the Lord.' And he worshiped the Lord there.'" (I Samuel 1:12-28)

Hannah kept her promise as well, and Elkanah honored it. That is how much he loved her. Elkanah was the head of the house and he had to approve it. God has His timing and we may not understand as we go through the trial, but based on His overwhelming and unconditional love for us, we just need to trust Him. The cross is explanation in itself as a reason to trust Him. "Trust in the Lord with all your heart and lean not on your own understanding; in all your ways submit to Him, and He will make your paths straight." (Proverbs 3:5-6)

Hannah persevered and never stopped praying.

Hannah's Prayer

"Then Hannah prayed and said: 'My heart rejoices in the Lord; in the Lord, my horn is lifted high. My mouth boasts over my enemies, for I delight in Your deliverance. 'There is no one holy like the Lord; there is no one besides You; there is no Rock like our God. 'Do not keep talking so proudly or let your mouth speak such arrogance, for the Lord is a God who knows, and by Him deeds are weighed. 'The bows of the warriors are broken, but those who stumbled are armed with strength. Those who were full hire themselves out for food, but those who were hungry are hungry no more. She who was barren has borne seven children, but she who has had many sons pines away. 'The Lord brings death and makes alive; He brings down to the grave and raises up. The Lord sends poverty and wealth; He humbles, and He exalts. He raises the poor from the dust and lifts the needy from the ash heap; He seats them with princes and has them inherit a throne of honor. 'For the foundations of the earth are the Lord's; on them He has set the world. He will guard the feet of His faithful servants, but the

wicked will be silenced in the place of darkness. 'It is not by strength that one prevails; those who oppose the Lord will be broken. The Most High will thunder from heaven; the Lord will judge the ends of the earth. 'He will give strength to His king and exalt the horn of His anointed.' Then Elkanah went home to Ramah, but the boy ministered before the Lord under Eli the priest." (I Samuel 2:1-11)

I kept writing even though my books had not been published and even though at times I knew my family did not believe I would be published. I knew, and that was all that mattered. People may not believe in the dreams that God places in their hearts, but that does not matter. All that matters is God's promise to fulfill it. I began writing the year my son died in 2000 and have kept writing ever since then. The titles, the path of each book, and the words all come. I was finally published in 2013 and at this time, this book is book number 23. God is so faithful. Never doubt Him. "I thank my God every time I remember you. In all my prayers for all of you, I always pray with joy because of your partnership in the gospel from the first day until now, being confident of this, that He who began a good work in you will carry it on to completion until the day of Christ Jesus." (Philippians 1:3-6)

God wants to birth something in you as well. Will you stay faithful? Will you persevere through the trials? Your dream, the passion He may want to birth in and through you may be a family, it may be children, to become a singer, or a ministry. Maybe it is a new job in which you can be a light and a testimony to those in the workplace. Will you let Him? Will you see it through? You may not see all the people your witness may touch, but God does.

I moved back to Texas, after several back-and-forth trips between Texas and South Carolina. The last time I moved back was at the end of 2008. It took me a little while to find a church that felt like home, one where I could feel the presence of the Holy Spirit, but I finally found one and began going to it at the end of 2009. This is where I met Pat (Patricia) Williams; she was a light, and pure in heart and spirit. She also had cancer, but she did not make that known. She did not want to be known as someone who had cancer. By her life-witness, she wanted to be known as a child of the King. It was evident.

When I moved back to Texas, I did not have a car, so I borrowed one or got rides until I was finally able to purchase one. Pat always volunteered to give me a ride to church, even though I was not exactly on the way to church. She always volunteered to help around the church and was always available to pray. It wasn't just at church or around her friends. She was a light at work also. During her last days, she still showed her light, and people knew she was a Christian. There were many stories from people she worked with being told at her funeral. Pat made a difference and her light within touched many people, including myself. She finally passed away in 2011, and her life still touches all those who remember her. The cancer was a hard and painful battle, but she did not allow it to define her – God did – and she did not have to declare her faith – she lived it. She always had a smile on her face even in her last days; she had an inner beauty that shined brightly on the outside.

How do you wear your trial? Can people look at you and tell or do you show your faith in God to get you through it and wear a look of joy? You do not have to be a minister, a singer, an evangelist, or a writer to make a difference. You just have to say "yes" to God and surrender to His will. He will do the rest as you allow His Holy Spirit to work through you. His Holy Spirit will touch people regardless of the occupation or position in life you possess.

Hannah's love for the Lord was quite evident in her prayer, and her barrenness did not define her either; rather, her love for the Lord shined through as she pursued Him and the answer to her prayer. When the Lord answers your prayer or uses your life to touch others, it should leave you in a state of awe and wonder of God. Awe that God Almighty should use any of us; it is humbling.

Mary felt that same awe as she treasured and pondered everything that had just happened in her heart; she gave birth to Jesus, the Son of God.

"And there were shepherds living out in the fields nearby, keeping watch over their flocks at night. An angel of the Lord appeared to them, and the glory of the Lord shone around them, and they were terrified.

But the angel said to them, 'Do not be afraid. I bring you good news that will cause great joy for all the people. Today in the town of David a Savior has been born to you; He is the Messiah, the Lord. This will be a sign to you: You will find a baby wrapped in cloths and lying in a manger.' Suddenly a great company of the heavenly host appeared with the angel, praising God and saying, 'Glory to God in the highest heaven, and on earth peace to those on whom His favor rests.' When the angels had left them and gone into heaven, the shepherds said to one another, 'Let's go to Bethlehem and see this thing that has happened, which the Lord has told us about.' So, they hurried off and found Mary and Joseph, and the baby, who was lying in the manger. When they had seen Him, they spread the word concerning what had been told them about this child, and all who heard it were amazed at what the shepherds said to them. But Mary treasured up all these things and pondered them in her heart. The shepherds returned, glorifying and praising God for all the things they had heard and seen, which were just as they had been told." (Luke 2:8-20)

What does God want to birth in you? Is there a "Samuel" waiting to be born in you? Will you go through the trial to allow God to use you? He will be with you every step of the way; trust Him.

"But now, this is what the Lord says—He who created you, Jacob, He who formed you, Israel: 'Do not fear, for I have redeemed you; I have summoned you by name; you are Mine. When you pass through the waters, I will be with you; and when you pass through the rivers, they will not sweep over you. When you walk through the fire, you will not be burned; the flames will not set you ablaze. For I am the Lord your God, the Holy One of Israel, your Savior; I give Egypt for your ransom, Cush and Seba in your stead. Since you are precious and honored in My sight, and because I love you, I will give people in exchange for you, nations in exchange for your life. Do not be afraid, for I am with you; I will bring your children from the east and gather you from the west. I will say to the north, 'Give them up!' and to the south, 'Do not hold them back.' Bring My sons from afar and My daughters from the ends of the earth—everyone who is called by My name, whom I created for My glory, whom I formed and made.'" (Isaiah 43:1-7)

10

Purpose

Finally! You made it! Year after year, trial after trial, you have transitioned into your dream, your purpose, and the answer to your prayers. But the difficulty is not quite over. There will still be learning curves and circumstances will arise in which you will need to use what you learned through the trials. Oh, and then there is Satan, he will not allow you to flow freely in your purpose and make a difference for God without trying to hinder you or make you fall. That is why the trial took so long, God is a good Father and He will not allow you to pass through to your purpose without equipping you with everything you will need to stay in it.

It will be a time of pure joy! When you are doing something you are called to do, your heart and spirit will feel more alive than at any other time. But there will be new learning curves. Using what you have learned, you will face new challenges. You will have opportunities to grow in your spiritual discernment, like Samuel. Learn to listen with your heart, with your spirit, and to fine-tune your spiritual hearing. As Samuel grew up under the tutelage of Eli, he had to learn the voice of God. Up to now, he had heard Eli but when God spoke to him, it was new. He had Eli there to help him, and God will have people in your in your new position to help you grow even more.

The Lord Calls Samuel

"The boy Samuel ministered before the Lord under Eli. In those days the word of the Lord was rare; there were not many visions. One night Eli, whose eyes were becoming so weak that he could barely see, was lying down in his usual place. The lamp of God had not yet gone out, and Samuel was lying down in the house of the Lord, where the ark of God was. Then the Lord called Samuel. Samuel answered, 'Here I am.' And he ran to Eli and said, 'Here I am; you called me.' But Eli said, 'I did not call; go back and lie down.' So, he went and lay. Again, the Lord called, 'Samuel!' And Samuel got up and went to Eli and said, 'Here I am; you called me.'

'My son,' Eli said, 'I did not call; go back and lie down.' Now Samuel did not yet know the Lord: The word of the Lord had not yet been revealed to him. A third time the Lord called, 'Samuel!' And Samuel got up and went to Eli and said, 'Here I am; you called me.' Then Eli realized that the Lord was calling the boy. So Eli told Samuel, 'Go and lie down, and if he calls you, say, 'Speak, Lord, for your servant is listening." So, Samuel went and lay down in his place. The Lord came and stood there, calling as at the other times, 'Samuel! Samuel!' Then Samuel said, 'Speak, for your servant is listening.'" (I Samuel 3:1-10)

There will be new things God wants to teach you, and it will be even more exciting in this new learning phase. Before, it was learning to examine yourself, the sins you committed, repenting, the things you needed to do or not do, and ways to step out of your comfort zone. You learned ways to overcome the trials you were facing in order to grow closer to deliverance. Now, He will add more in order to equip you with more of what you need for your new position.

Samuel had to learn to be bold in speaking the truth of what God was telling him, using spiritual discernment to know when to speak it. In hearing the Lord's voice, he had to learn obedience and be quick to obey. It was his time to blossom as the Lord's vessel. In all the things you will be learning in this new phase of your life, it will be exhilarating! It is your time to blossom!

Samuel grew and learned more and more and became recognized by the people of the land as a prophet of the Lord. "The Lord was with

Samuel as he grew up, and he let none of Samuel's words fall to the ground. And all Israel from Dan to Beersheba recognized that Samuel was attested as a prophet of the Lord. The Lord continued to appear at Shiloh, and there He revealed Himself to Samuel through His word." (I Samuel 3:19-21)

Samuel was a miracle child, Hannah was barren for so long and God finally answered her prayers. As God began to use Samuel, he had to step out in faith and in the authority of who God had called him to be, trusting it was God and obey what He commanded him to do. "The righteous will live by faith." (Galatians 3:11) And that takes action. "So too, faith by itself, if it is not complemented by action, is dead. But someone will say, 'You have faith; I have deeds.' Show me your faith without deeds, and I will show you my faith by my deeds." (James 2:17-18) If you want to grow in the new position God has called you to then you too, will have to step out in faith, you move first then the way gets cleared. "Now the Jordan is at flood stage all during harvest. Yet as soon as the priests who carried the ark reached the Jordan and their feet touched the water's edge, the flowing water stood still. It backed up as far upstream as Adam, a city in the area of Zarethan, while the water flowing toward the Sea of the Arabah (the Salt Sea) was completely cut off. So, the people crossed over opposite Jericho." (Joshua 3:15-16)

As a child of God, you have the authority to step and do what He has called you to do, "When Jesus had called the Twelve together, He gave them power and authority to drive out all demons and to cure diseases, and he sent them out to proclaim the kingdom of God and to heal the sick." (Luke 9:1-2) If He commands you to do it, then He will also back you up, "And I will do whatever you ask in my name, so that the Father may be glorified in the Son. If you ask Me anything in My name, I will do it." (John 14:13-14)

Eli was a priest, and his sons were not handling the offerings with respect and reverence for the Lord. Eli warned them, but it was left there, and they continued. God had to "clean house," and He did that through an ongoing issue with the Philistines. When God cleaned house, He moved Samuel into the role of priest and he made sacrifices on behalf of the people. He was trained by Eli who took over for him after his death. Samuel had Ephramite blood, "There was a certain man from Ramathaim, a Zuphite from the hill country of Ephraim, whose name was Elkanah son of Jeroham, the son of Elihu, the son of Tohu, the son of Zuph, an Ephraimite." (I Samuel 1:1) He was a Levite: "These are the men David put in charge of the music in the house of the Lord after the ark came to rest there. They ministered with music before the Tabernacle, the tent of meeting, until Solomon built the temple of the Lord in Jerusalem. They performed their duties according to the regulations laid down for them. Here are the men who served, together with their sons: From the Kohathites: Heman, the musician, the son of Joel, the son of **Samuel**, the son of Elkanah, the son of Jeroham, the son of Eliel, the son of Toah, the son of Zuph, the son of **Elkanah**." (I Chronicles 6:31-35)

Samuel was known to be the first of the prophets, "Indeed, beginning with Samuel, all the prophets who have spoken have foretold these days." (Acts 3:24) Samuel was the last of the judges and the first to anoint kings. The days of having a king began under Samuel's ministry. He obeyed God, he trusted him, and he honored God and God showed him favor and gave him authority. When we put God first, when our heart is for God, all of this will fall into place. Samuel never sought the roles he was placed in, he was a prophet and a prophet is chosen by God and he hears from God and proclaims the will of God. Samuel stepped right into this role as well as the other ones and he honored them and served in those roles in reverence to God. What is ahead for you as you step out in faith, obeying God and showing Him the glory and honor due His holy name? Samuel blossomed in the office of prophet, priest, and judge because his heart was faithful to God.

The Philistines had been oppressing the Israelites when Samuel began his leadership and at one point at the beginning of his ministry, they had captured the Ark of the Lord.

Upon arrival at the Philistine camp, they broke out in tumors and a great panic arose. They knew it was Israel's God and made plans to give the Ark back. One of the reasons for the oppression of the Philistines was the continued roller coaster faith and obedience of the Israelites. God would allow it to open their eyes and get them to return to Him. When the Ark had been captured by the Israelites it upset them, and when it was returned, all the people returned to the Lord. But their issue with the Philistines was not over. Samuel went before the Lord and prayed. The Lord was with them and the Philistines were subdued when they tried to attack Israel.

"Then all the people of Israel turned back to the Lord. So, Samuel said to all the Israelites, 'If you are returning to the Lord with all your hearts, then rid yourselves of the foreign gods and the Ashtoreths and commit yourselves to the Lord and serve Him only, and He will deliver you out of the hand of the Philistines.' So, the Israelites put away their Baals and Ashtoreths and served the Lord only. Then Samuel said, 'Assemble all Israel at Mizpah, and I will intercede with the Lord for you.' When they had assembled at Mizpah, they drew water and poured it out before the Lord. On that day they fasted and there they confessed, 'We have sinned against the Lord.' Now Samuel was serving as leader of Israel at Mizpah. When the Philistines heard that Israel had assembled at Mizpah, the rulers of the Philistines came up to attack them. When the Israelites heard of it, they were afraid because of the Philistines. They said to Samuel, 'Do not stop crying out to the Lord our God for us, that he may rescue us from the hand of the Philistines.' Then Samuel took a suckling lamb and sacrificed it as a whole burnt offering to the Lord. He cried out to the Lord on Israel's behalf, and the Lord answered him.

While Samuel was sacrificing the burnt offering, the Philistines drew near to engage Israel in battle. But that day the Lord thundered with loud thunder against the Philistines and threw them into such a panic that they were routed before the Israelites. The men of Israel rushed out of Mizpah and pursued the Philistines, slaughtering them along the way to a point below Beth Kar. Then Samuel took a stone and set it up between Mizpah and Shen. He named it Ebenezer, saying, 'Thus far the Lord has helped us.' So, the Philistines were subdued, and they stopped invading Israel's territory. Throughout Samuel's lifetime, the hand of the Lord was against the Philistines. The towns from Ekron to Gath that the Philistines had captured from Israel were restored to Israel, and Israel delivered the neighboring territory from the hands of the Philistines. And there was peace between Israel and the Amorites.

Samuel continued as Israel's leader all the days of his life. From year to year, he went on a circuit from Bethel to Gilgal to Mizpah, judging Israel in all those places. But he always went back to Ramah, where his home was, and there he also held court for Israel. And he built an altar there to the Lord." (I Samuel 7:2-17)

What does God have in store for you? Are you ready to surrender all and obey Him without question or doubt? Will you step out of your comfort zone in faith, that He can show Himself big through you and be glorified? To do anything for the Lord takes faith that He will use it for His glory. Just make sure you keep your heart pure with a sincere faith and devotion to God. As you begin to grow in your new destiny, Satan will try to tempt you into liking the praises of men. Always remember who you are doing it for God Almighty. "So, whether you eat or drink or whatever you do, do it all for the glory of God." (I Corinthians 10:31) God is infinite, He has no limit, and what He will do through you will be limitless if you love Him with all of your heart, obey Him, keep Him first in your heart, even over your own wants and desires, and give Him the glory and honor due Him.

Is there a "Samuel" waiting to be born in you? Will you go through the trials with God trusting Him and not giving up? Your purpose in Him will be limitless and you will blossom.

"Very truly I tell you, whoever believes in Me will do the works I have been doing, and they will do even greater things than these because I am going to the Father. And I will do whatever you ask in My name, so that the Father may be glorified in the Son. You may ask Me for anything in My name, and I will do it. "If you love Me, keep My commands. And I will ask the Father, and He will give you another advocate to help you and be with you forever— the Spirit of truth. The world cannot accept Him, because it neither sees Him nor knows Him. But you know Him, for He lives with you and will be in you. I will not leave you as orphans; I will come to you. Before long, the world will not see me anymore, but you will

see Me. Because I live, you also will live. On that day you will realize that I am in my Father, and you are in Me, and I am in you. Whoever has My commands and keeps them is the one who loves Me. The one who loves Me will be loved by My Father, and I too will love them and show Myself to them." (John 14:12-21)

Final Thoughts

Hannah went from barren to blossoming in the purpose God had for her. She pursued God to bear a son. She had a child that God used abundantly to help her people. Hannah fell in love and was married, and naturally growing that love into a family would be next. Year after year Hannah and Elkanah tried to have children with no success. She did not let that stop her; it fueled her instead. Hannah became more and more determined to have a child, and this determination drew her closer to God. She sought Him through prayer more passionately; she did not give up or get angry, but instead fell to her knees.

"For I know the plans I have for you,' declares the Lord, 'plans to prosper you and not to harm you, plans to give you hope and a future. Then you will call on Me and come and pray to Me, and I will listen to you. You will seek Me and find Me when you seek Me with all your heart. I will be found by you,' declares the Lord, 'and will bring you back from captivity.'" (Jeremiah 29:11-14)

What would you do? What have you done when faced with one roadblock after another for a dream you are pursuing? Maybe it is something you are facing right now. Are you full of anger and self-pity? Has depression and despair taken over? It will consume you if you let it, you need to get stubborn and forge through as Hannah did; she wept but she became determined not to give up. It drew her closer to God, not away. How has your trial affected your relationship with God? Maybe reading this has changed your view of the trial and drawn you closer to God. Sometimes the trials that seem never-ending are for our protection and are a blessing in disguise from what the Lord wants to birth in and through us. "As you know, we count as blessed those who have persevered. You have heard of Job's perseverance and have seen what the Lord finally brought about. The Lord is full of compassion and mercy." (James 5:11)

Don't give up; a glorious adventure awaits as you learn to trust Him through the trial. Through it, He is equipping you with what you need for the adventure that awaits! He loves you and does not want you to proceed unprepared.

"Consider it pure joy, my brothers and sisters, whenever you face trials of many kinds, because you know that the testing of your faith produces perseverance. Let perseverance finish its work so that you may be mature and complete, not lacking anything. If any of you lacks wisdom, you should ask God, who gives generously to all without finding fault, and it will be given to you. But when you ask, you must believe and not doubt, because the one who doubts is like a wave of the sea, blown and tossed by the wind. That person should not expect to receive anything from the Lord. Such a person is double-minded and unstable in all they do." (James 1:2-8)

What will you allow God to take you through to birth something wonderful in you and through you? Don't give up; rely on His strength to see you through. You will reap a harvest!

"Let us not become weary in doing good, for at the proper time we will reap a harvest if we do not give up." (Galatians 6:9)

God bless you!
Sandra (Lott) Smith

Bibliography

Berry, M. (2018, July 18). (S. Lott, Interviewer) Hutto, Texas, United States.

Center, C.-L. M. (1993-2018). *chabad.org-7 blessings*. Retrieved from Chabad.org: https://www.chabad.org/library/article_cdo/aid/479965/jewish/Text-of-Sheva-Brachot.htm

Center, C.-L. M. (1993-2018). *Chabad. org--newlyweds*. Retrieved from Chabad.org: https://www.chabad.org/library/article_cdo/aid/476744/jewish/Newlyweds.htm

Center, C.-L. M. (1993-2018). *Chabad. org--wedding ceremony*. Retrieved from chabad.org:
https://www.chabad.org/library/article_cdo/aid/476757/jewish/Jewish-Wedding-Ceremony.htm

Webster. (1995). *Webster's New American Dictionary Webster's*. New York: Wiley Publishing Inc.

Wikipedia. (2018, June). *Wikipedia*. Retrieved July 7, 2018, from Wikipedia: https://en.wikipedia.org/wiki/Jewish_wedding

Wikipedia. (2018, June). *Wikipedia-Betrothal*. Retrieved July 7, 2018, from Wikipedia: https://en.wikipedia.org/wiki/Engagement

Wikipedia. (2018, July 7). *Wikipedia-Ketubah*. Retrieved July 21, 2018, from https://en.wikipedia.org/wiki/Ketubah

Wikipedia. (2018, February 9). *Wikipedia-Sheva Brachot*. Retrieved July 26, 2018, from Wikipedia-Sheva Brachot: https://en.wikipedia.org/wiki/Sheva_Brachot

Wikipedia. (2018, April 27). *Wikipedia--Tallit*. Retrieved July 26, 2018, from Wikipedia: https://en.wikipedia.org/wiki/Tallit

Wikipedia. (2018, June 28). *Wikipedia--views on Jewish marriage*. Retrieved from Wikipedia--views on Jewish marriage: https://en.wikipedia.org/wiki/Jewish_views_on_marriage

Wikipedia. (2018, June 28). *Wikipedia-Views on Jewish Weddings*. Retrieved July 21, 2018, from Wikipedia: https://en.wikipedia.org/wiki/Jewish_views_on_marriage

Special Invitation

I cannot close this book without giving you the awesome privilege of becoming a child of God, a chance to have every wrong made right and every sin washed away. If you have never asked Jesus into your heart, or maybe you did but you were never sincere, please pray the prayer on the pages following. It will be the best thing you have ever done.

After you do this, find a good Church to go to if you do not have one already. Fellowshipping with other Christians will help you on your new walk in Christ. It is also a place to worship God and learn more about Him. Also, tell someone! You must confess! This should be the happiest day of your life because you now know that your eternal home is in heaven!

I think that is the best life insurance anyone can have, and it is free!

(Romans 10:9-10) "That if you confess with your mouth, 'Jesus is Lord,' and believe in your heart that God raised Him from the dead, you will be saved. For it is with your heart that you believe and are justified, and it is with your mouth that you confess and are saved."

Congratulations and welcome to the family of God!

God Loves You!

(Jeremiah. 31:3) "I have loved you with an everlasting love; I have drawn you with loving-kindness."

I Timothy 2:3-4 "God our Savior, who wants all men to be saved and to come to the knowledge of the truth."

He will not knock on the door of your heart forever. Will you let Him in?

Revelation 3:20 "Here I am! I stand at the door and knock. If anyone hears My voice and opens the door, I will come in and eat with him, and he with Me."

Jesus is the only way to God.
John 14:6 "I am the way, the truth, and the life. No one comes to the Father except through Me."

John 3:3 "I tell you the truth, no one can see the kingdom of God unless he is born again."

And you must make Him Lord of your life.
Matthew 6:24 "No one can serve two masters."
Matthew 7:21 "Not everyone who says to Me, 'Lord, Lord', will enter the kingdom of heaven, but only he who does the will of My Father who is in heaven."

We must leave our old ways behind.
Mark 3:25 "If a house is divided against itself, that house cannot stand."

You can't live according to the flesh and desires of the sinful nature and expect to have Jesus in your heart. He is holy. He is love. Love and Hate cannot exist together.

Ephesians 4:22-24 "You were taught, with regard to your former way of life, to put off your old self, which is being corrupted by its deceitful desires; to be made new in the attitude of your minds; and to put on the new self, created to be like God in true righteousness and holiness."

God gives you the ability to do His will. He knows it is hard.
Philippians 4:13 "I can do everything through Him who gives me strength."

Romans 3:23 "For all have sinned and fall short of the glory of God."

I John 1:9 "If we confess our sins, He is faithful and just and will forgive us our sins and purify us from all unrighteousness."

John 1:12 "Yet to all who received Him, to those who believed in His name, He gave the right to become children of God."

Romans 10:10 "For it is with your heart that you believe and are justified, and it is with your mouth that you confess and are saved."

Then after you confess and ask forgiveness and receive Jesus into your heart, you must testify (tell someone) and be baptized. In this, God is glorified, and others might be saved by your example.

II Timothy 1:8 "So do not be ashamed to testify about our Lord"

I Peter 3:21 "And this water symbolizes baptism that now saves you also- not the removal of dirt from the body but the pledge of a good conscience toward God. It saves you by the resurrection of Jesus Christ."

Invitation To Salvation Prayer

Dear Almighty Father in heaven, I know that I am a sinner and I ask your forgiveness of all my sins. I want to make You the Lord of my life and I want to serve You all the days of my life. I believe that Jesus Christ died on the cross for my sins.

Thank you so much for loving me, and waiting on me to come to the knowledge of the truth! Thank you for my salvation. Please help me and guide me in learning your Word so I can be a light to the world. Please, Jesus, come into my heart, and baptize me with your Holy Spirit. I thank You and praise Your Holy Name and ask all this in the name of Jesus Christ our Lord. Amen.

Other Books by Sandra (Lott) Smith

Adult Books

Jeremy's Journey
Safe In Papa's Hands
Her Final Curtain
Deep Waters Within
Deep Waters Rage: Sequel to Deep Waters Within
My Father's Eyes: Seeing Yourself Through The Eyes of Love
Ride the Wind
An Eagle's Flight
A Princess in Waiting
The Princess in the Harlot
Step By Step Into A Deeper Walk In Christ
I'm Saved! Where Do I Go From Here?
The Day Hope Was Born: God's Gift of Love
The Holy Spirit and the Baptism of the Holy Spirit
Repairing Broken Walls: Restoring Joy & Peace-The Book
Repairing Broken Walls: Restoring Joy & Peace-The Study Guide
Jewels From the Word & Manna For the Soul
Captivated By God's Love: Poems From the Heart
You've Got This: Learning To Let Go
I'm Saved! What Next? Beginning Your Walk In Christ
The Father He Never Knew He Needed
In the Garden with Jesus
Princess Anastasia & the Kingdom of Divulgence

Children's Books

The Sheep That Went Astray
Naomi's Joy
Molly's Journey to Forgiveness
Tim & Gerald Ray Series: The Wind Has a Voice
Tim & Gerald Ray Series: How Did He Get in There?
Tim & Gerald Ray Series: A Light in the Sky
Tim & Gerald Ray Series: Let's Go Swimming
Tim & Gerald Ray Series: Blowing in the Wind
Tim & Gerald Ray Series: Summer on Grandma's Farm
Sassy Goes Exploring

Sandra (Lott) Smith was born and raised in San Antonio, Texas, with one sister and two brothers. Sandra loves the mountains, making candles, and jewelry. She is the author of Jeremy's Journey, Deep Waters Within, A Princess in Waiting, Ride the Wind, and more. She has also written children's such as, The Wind Has a Voice and How Did He Get in There, Molly's Journey to Forgiveness, and more. She has written over 38 books to date and began writing poetry as soon as she was saved in June 1998. The Lord gave her, her first book to write right after her son was killed. Writing was not something she sought out. She poured her heart into time spent with the Lord in order to allow Him to heal her heart and the name of her first book was birthed in her spirit along with the chapters and what it was to be about during a devotion time. It was called: God's Love; ironically enough, with all that she was going through, God's love was exactly what she needed.

She is passionate about studying the Bible. She has taught Sunday school, and Bible Study Groups, assists in preaching in her present church, and served in the Celebrate Recovery Ministry, and Homeless Outreach. Sandra was also interviewed on radio shows such as Golden Life Living and WMAP Radio (World's Most Amazing People based out of New York), the Bill Martinez show, and a Fox Radio show called the Kim Kennedy Show.

She is a devoted mother of 2 sons (Tim & Gerald Ray), Gerald Ray the youngest, has gone on to be with the Lord due to a car accident. Through the death of her youngest son at the age of 16, a rocky marriage to an alcoholic and the abuse that came with that, and other overwhelming trials, she has drawn close to the loving arms of the Father. Experiencing God's unconditional love as He held her heart in His hands, has created a passion in her to help others grow in their understanding of and receive God's love and grow spiritually. She has the heart to help hurting women discover the princess in Christ that they truly are and overcome abuse. She teaches on topics to help you reach spiritual maturity, persevere through the hard times, and how to reach your destiny in Christ!